SOME TENDENCIES IN BRITISH THEOLOGY

JOHN KENNETH MOZLEY

Some Tendencies in
British Theology

SOME TENDENCIES IN BRITISH THEOLOGY

From the publication of *Lux Mundi*
to the present day

by

THE LATE JOHN KENNETH MOZLEY, D.D.

LONDON

S · P · C · K

1952

First published in 1951
Reprinted, 1952
by S.P.C.K.
Northumberland Avenue, London, W.C.2
Printed in Great Britain by
Billing and Sons Ltd., Guildford and Esher

ACKNOWLEDGMENTS

The quotation on p. 80 from the chapter " The Future of the Evangelical Movement," by E. W. Barnes, in *Liberal Evangelicalism, An Interpretation*, is given by permission of Messrs. Hodder and Stoughton; that on p. 151 from *The Place of Jesus Christ in Modern Christianity*, by J. Baillie, by permission of Messrs. T. and T. Clark; that on p. 162 from *Grace and Personality*, by J. Oman, by permission of the Cambridge University Press.

CONTENTS

NOTE

When our brother, Kenneth Mozley, died this book was nearly but not quite completely finished. This may explain the possible omission of names of theologians which the reader might expect to find, and it is hoped that allowance will be made.

We owe our grateful thanks to the Dean of Winchester, Dr. Selwyn, for his Preface, to Dr. J. F. Mozley for his editorship of the manuscript, and last but not least to the Society for Promoting Christian Knowledge for their kindness and courtesy in arranging for the publication of the book.

E. N. MOZLEY.

ELEANOR SPILMONT.

PREFACE

I HAVE been asked to write a brief Preface to this book on the score of a friendship with the author which covered over forty years and was as bright at the end as at the beginning. The qualities which made Kenneth Mozley stand out among his fellows at Cambridge, both as an undergraduate and as a junior don, remained with him throughout life. Few men were better company than he, whether in social intercourse or in the cut and thrust of debate at the Union or on a committee; his vigorous intellect and force of character were alike salted with wit and sweetened by an abounding charity; no mean or unfair word crossed his lips, for no such thought was allowed to lodge in his mind. His ardent Liberalism in politics sprang from a profound conviction that every man should have his due and a deep compassion for those whom society treated most hardly. And with it went a pervading piety, not worn on his sleeve but governing his whole life, shaped primarily by his home traditions (he was a kinsman of Cardinal Newman), nourished by his study of the Bible, and refreshed and widened by familiarity with the writings of divines of all ages and of all Christian denominations.

He left no one in doubt of his own resolute and undeviating Churchmanship, and perhaps for that very reason had many friends who were not Anglicans; indeed it would be difficult to say whether Bishop Gore or Principal Forsyth among the writers of that time exercised the greater influence on his thought.

It has often been said that Kenneth Mozley's theological books are difficult to understand, and the element of truth in this is surprising, since it is in sharp contrast to his conversation, where the deepest or most tangled issues were often illuminated in a sentence or two. Part of the truth is explained by the nature of the tasks to which he set himself. His early book, *The Doctrine of the Atonement* (1915), was a historical study of Christian thought upon the Cross from the earliest times to the present century, in little more than 200 pages; and it could not be other than highly condensed. Again, the book he wrote for the

7

Doctrinal Commission, *The Impassibility of God* (1926), covers a highly technical field which was almost untrodden in English theology before. Yet I do not think that the charge of difficulty could be brought against *The Beginnings of Christian Theology* (1931), or his essay on " Grace and Freedom " in *Essays Catholic and Critical* (1926). Parts of them need to be read twice, but that is little more than to say that they are real theology and no mere surface stuff, and the effect of such attention is that the reader's mind is trained and strengthened to face the calls, moral as well as intellectual, that Christianity makes upon it. He had not the gift of popular appeal which belonged to Gore or Inge; but it may be surmised that as " a teacher of teachers " his work will last not less long than theirs and prove continuously fruitful in the Church's life.

His friends will certainly hope so. They themselves have the joyful recollection of his vivid and affectionate personality, his trenchant sayings often loudly uttered, his playing of fives or chess, his laughter, the courage with which he bore his asthma, his transparent goodness. But they will wish also that those who did not know him may catch, through his books, including this posthumous volume now published, something of his thought and of the accents in which he imparted it. It is no accident that so many of his books have dedications—" To the memory of my mother," " To my colleagues of the Archbishops' Doctrinal Commission," " To my wife, for all that this book owes to her and for all that I owe besides "—for his relationships to others were ever present in his work. But always above all stood his— and their—relationship to God. The closing paragraphs of his book on the Atonement are characteristic.

" The Atonement, as fact and doctrine, should evoke feelings not only of respect and self-surrender but of worship. The *Lex Credendi* should be also the *Lex Adorandi*. That Eucharistic Worship which is to many the highest possible expression of their adoration of God is the worship of the Crucified even more than of the Incarnate Christ. . . . We worship Him for what He is, and in that which He is lies that which He has done. And that which He has done He did first unto God by victory over sin through the gateway of seeming defeat, by breaking that chain of guilt which bound down the noblest and most God-like part of God's creation, by the establishment of the new Kingdom grounded in holiness and sacrificial love. This is the fruit of His death, and this the secret of the Adoration of the Lamb.''

Kenneth Mozley died with the latest task that he had set himself unfinished. He had intended to write a book entitled *Tendencies in British Theology from the publication of '' Lux Mundi '' to the Present Day*—that is, to the day when he passed his manuscript to the printer. In fact, he had neither examined all the tendencies, nor covered all the years from the publication of *Lux Mundi* to his own death. But what he had written was no mere draft. It was finished work—as finished as any of his published work. Consequently, although the book which he planned was—to our loss— never completed, we have here a large number of the studies of which it would have consisted, and which are no less valuable in themselves because the plan in which they were comprised was never carried out.

E. G. SELWYN.

INTRODUCTION

IN the year 1882 Edward Bouverie Pusey, Regius Professor of Hebrew in the University of Oxford and Canon of Christ Church, died at the age of eighty-two. It was nearly fifty years since John Keble had preached that " Assize Sermon " which John Henry Newman regarded as the beginning of the Tractarian Movement. They had been years of great change, marked by events of dramatic character and by storms of intense controversy. And whatever assessment may be made of the Tractarian Movement, it was without question largely due to it that the Church of England in 1882 was in many ways very different from what it had been in 1833. On no man had that half-century weighed so heavily as upon Pusey. From 1845, when Newman was received into the Church of Rome, Pusey had been the very head and front of the Movement. For more reasons than one the stress of the times left the venerated Keble in comparative peace in his country vicarage at Hursley. But Pusey was continuously in the thick of the battle. As we look back, it is extraordinary to realize that this Oxford Professor, so eminently the scholar and theologian, so lacking in the popular gifts which are normally to be found in the leader of a great cause, probably aroused more furious antipathy and engaged more intense devotion than any other man in England—a fact yet more remarkable when we remember that it was the age of Disraeli and Gladstone in politics, and of Carlyle, Ruskin, Tennyson, and Browning in literature. By the time of his death Pusey had lived down the more violent manifestations of hostility which had been directed against him. Not in Tractarian and High Church circles alone had he become a *clarum et venerabile nomen*. At his funeral Mr. Gladstone, then Prime Minister, and Lord Salisbury, who was soon to succeed to that great office, were two of the pall-bearers.

Those who cast their eyes over the years that had passed must have thought of Pusey's death as marking in some way the close of an era. What they cannot equally have realized was that a door now began to open upon a new era that was deeply to affect the whole character of religious thought in England, and also, with the necessary reservations, in Scotland, and to lead on towards a situation very different from that which then existed. While Pusey lived, that was, I think it may be said, impossible. For there was no challenging his supremacy within the High Church party, as that party had been revived and its theological and ecclesiastical positions re-ordered through the influence of the Tractarian Movement. And though in 1882 the High Church party was not dominant within the Church of England, it was no longer, as it may well have appeared to be in the middle of the century, a party maintaining a precarious existence within a body that was consistently suspicious and, on occasions, inclined to be definitely hostile.

It is desirable that Pusey's theological position should be briefly expounded. He was a Hebraist and a Biblical scholar of pronouncedly conservative outlook and opinions. In his youth he had made acquaintance with the scholarship of Germany, and had written a book which was regarded as showing an unduly sympathetic attitude to the critical tendencies which had appeared in that country. He himself came to look back upon it with disfavour, and never again did he diverge from a strictly conservative position. His best-known work in Biblical scholarship was a course of lectures on the Book of Daniel, in which he massed the arguments for the traditional date and authorship of the Book, in opposition to the ascription of it to an unknown author of the age of the Maccabees. He may not have committed himself in so many words to the doctrine of the verbal inerrancy of Holy Scripture, but his outlook was consonant with that doctrine and hardly with any other. Under his leadership the High Church party was as resolutely opposed as were the Evangelicals to the first appearances of what came to be known as the Higher Criticism. In opposition to the volume entitled *Essays and Reviews*, which was published in 1860, Pusey stood with his cousin, the famous philanthropist and Evangelical layman, Lord Shaftesbury. It is not a book that would now be regarded as subversive or even surprising; but in the middle of the last century it caused a great sensation, and it did in point of fact involve a wider break with the traditional position in respect of the Bible and theology than any previous volume that had come from within the Church of England.

" Pusey reverenced the Bible as supreme ": so some twenty

years after the Professor's death wrote that stalwart Evangelical
Sir Robert Anderson, who shared none of Pusey's characteristic
views in matters ecclesiastical. But Pusey did not isolate the
Bible in the way in which it may not unfairly be said the Evangelicals tended to do. His theology was Biblical—but also patristic.
He was a patristic scholar of profound learning, and it was from
his study of the Fathers that he came to, and afterwards defended,
the Tractarian position. His doctrinal writings, such as those
on the sacraments, and the reply to Farrar on the eschatological
question, which bore the name *What is of faith as to everlasting
punishment?*, are full of quotations from the Fathers. The history
of doctrine never seems to have presented any problems to
him. He read it as a straightforward story with truth on the
one side and heresy on the other. His theology of the Church
was in line with that which had been pursued with increasing
confidence by the Tractarians, with their stress upon the doctrine
of the apostolical succession as ensuring the link between the
Church of their day and the primitive Church, and the validity
of the Holy Orders derived through the episcopal succession
from the apostles. Where Pusey never varied, as compared
with Newman and the others who went to Rome, was in his
conviction that the Church of England belonged to the true
Church of Christ and possessed all that was necessary for the
due ordering of its life. He was at no time " anti-Roman "
in the way that was once the case with Newman, but he rejected
without any vacillation of spirit the exclusive claims made for
the Church and See of Rome. There is, equally, no reason
to suppose that he was in any way intellectually disturbed by
the fact of the existence of the non-episcopal communions.
So far as one can say, they constituted no problem for him. They
were not part of the Church Catholic, true though it assuredly
was that members of them were not left destitute of the grace
of God.

It means no underrating of the work that Pusey did, of the
steadying influence which his firm hold upon historic Christianity
exerted, and of that single-mindedness of Christian life to which
R. W. Dale paid tribute in his declaration that he rose from the
reading of Pusey's *Life* with a deep conviction of his personal
greatness, if one finds it necessary to allow that Pusey gave
little of positive help to the end of the nineteenth century

and the beginning of the twentieth in the way of constructive thinking. For problems were coming in apace which demanded a treatment different from anything that Pusey himself gave to them, or that those who remained most profoundly under his influence could give. There were real issues to be faced, problems of Biblical criticism, of dogmatic theology, of the philosophy of religion, and of Christian unity and reunion. Whatever the upshot of the investigation of such problems might be, it was certain that they could neither be left on one side nor decided simply in accordance with Pusey's presuppositions. It was equally certain that crises would arise that would affect the whole religious situation, and that controversies would develop on a much wider field than that which had opened out as an immediate result of the Tractarian Movement. What could not have been foreseen was that the most influential book to appear within the decade after Dr. Pusey's death, and one destined to mark the beginnings of a new era in the Church of England in respect both of Biblical and of doctrinal concep- tions, would come from within the High Church party, and would have as its Editor, and as the writer of the article that was to cause the greatest stir, the Principal of that Pusey House which had been founded in Oxford in honour of Pusey, and as a witness to those theological principles specially associated with his name. The first edition of *Lux Mundi* saw the light in 1889. To no one did it come as a greater shock than to H. P. Liddon, the famous preacher, who was of all the theologians of his time the most faithful adherent to the principles and teaching of Dr. Pusey. With his death in 1890 the original Tractarian tradition, as a unity of religious principle, outlook, and interpretation, may be said to have come to an end. The dominant figure in Anglican High Churchmanship for the next forty years was to be Charles Gore.

But before *Lux Mundi* saw the light, there were influences powerfully affecting the world of Biblical and theological scholarship of which a word must be said. The "Higher Criticism," to give it its usual though not quite happy title, had advanced far beyond anything that had appeared in *Essays and Reviews*. The tradition concerning the provenance, authors, and dates of the books of the Old Testament had been replaced, in the writings of German scholars such as Wellhausen and

Kuenen, by a view which gave priority to many of the prophetic writings as compared with the Pentateuch, denied that the Pentateuch was the work of Moses and that David had written the Psalms, and led to important changes of outlook on the history and theology of Israel. In particular, the idea of a comprehensive monotheism taught by Moses and embodied in the Book of Deuteronomy was exchanged for a conception of a slowly forming monotheistic creed, which was first expressed in the writings of the Prophets of the eighth century, and did not gain full control over the thought of Israel till after the return from the exile. To a large extent this reconstruction depended upon literary analysis of the Pentateuchal writings; and the signs " J," " E," and " P " began to be used. It was in the late 70's and the 80's that this approach to the Old Testament began to influence British Biblical scholarship and to be expounded by those who accepted it. The lectures entitled *The Old Testament in the Jewish Church*, by W. Robertson Smith, may be taken as the sign of the beginning of a new era. They were delivered to public audiences in Scotland during the spring of 1881, after the controversy which had broken out with regard to his opinions had compelled him to withdraw from the ordinary work of his chair in Aberdeen. In his preface to the first edition of these lectures Robertson Smith remarked that " it is of the first importance that the reader should realize that Biblical criticism is not the invention of modern scholars, but the legitimate interpretation of historical facts." And of such criticism he claimed that " its great value " was that it " makes the Old Testament more real to us." But some years were to pass before the Higher Criticism of the Old Testament gained a firm hold on the minds of Biblical scholars within the Church of England.

In New Testament studies the famous Cambridge Three were still the dominant figures. Lightfoot indeed had gone to the See of Durham in 1879, and his main work on the New Testament, especially on the Epistles of St. Paul, lay behind him. But Westcott was Regius Professor of Divinity at Cambridge all through the 80's, and in 1881 he and Hort produced the great work, *The New Testament in Greek*, in which the text of the New Testament, as reconstructed in accordance with the principles they had followed, was set forth, and the principles themselves explained. In 1882 Westcott's commentary on St. John appeared in the " Speaker's Bible," to be followed in the course of the next few years by other commentaries on New Testament books. Hort himself, whom some would judge to have been the greatest of the three, produced very little; but in Cambridge, where he was successively Hulsean and Lady Margaret Professor, his influence has been described as " that of a master." He died in 1892: Westcott had succeeded Lightfoot as Bishop of Durham in 1890.

The Cambridge scholars represented a transitional stage in the study of the New Testament. So far as textual research and conclusions went, their influence was contrary to the conservatism which held to the *Textus Receptus* embodied in the Authorized Version as the truth of Scripture—that is, as a faithful reproduction of the words which at the first the sacred writers had put down. To take but three instances: the Westcott-Hort revision had no place for the last twelve verses of St. Mark as part of the original Marcan Gospel, nor for the first eleven verses of the eighth chapter of St. John as properly belonging to the fourth Gospel, nor for the sentence with regard to the Three Heavenly Witnesses as forming part of the true text of the seventh verse of the fifth chapter of the First Epistle of St. John. Moreover, from the historical point of view, Lightfoot's commentaries on some of St. Paul's Epistles broke new ground. On the other hand, on questions of authorship and literary criticism, especially with regard to the Gospels, they did not anticipate the new lines of study which were soon to become more and more common among scholars. Westcott's edition of St. John's Gospel is entirely conservative. There is no kind of envisaging of the possibility that the evangelist may not always be giving the *ipsissima verba* of Christ, and Westcott's " oral theory " of the Gospels allows of no literary interdependence of the synoptic writers, nor of any use of St. Mark by the first and third evangelists, nor of a second literary source, commonly called Q, on which the first and third evangelists may have drawn for their knowledge of the sayings of the Lord. Scholars who followed close afterwards, such as Swete and Stanton and Sanday and Armitage Robinson, became the sponsors of an account of Gospel origins which still remains, among non-Roman Catholic scholars, in possession of the field. More

recent theories, particularly those which come under the heading
of " Form-criticism," have sought to penetrate into methods
of compilation which may lie behind the written texts of our
Gospels, but they have not discarded that theory of the relations
existing between the synoptic Gospels which is sometimes
spoken of as " the two-document theory."

One other book of first-rate importance for the student of
theology saw the light at the end of the 80's. In 1888 Dr.
Edwin Hatch, the Reader in Ecclesiastical History in the University of Oxford, delivered his Hibbert Lectures on *The Influence
of Greek Ideas and Usages upon the Christian Church.* After his
death the lectures were edited by Dr. Fairbairn, the powerful
Scottish theologian who had become the first Principal of
Mansfield College, Oxford. The theme of Hatch's work is
apparent in the title; its tendency was to suggest that the original
nature of the Christian Gospel had been greatly changed owing
to the pressure of Greek philosophical and theological conceptions, with the concomitant terminology which was employed
by Christian thinkers. The importance of Hatch's work was
seen and emphasized by Harnack, whose *History of Dogma* in
its first edition was published in 1886-9. In course of time it
was translated into English, and in the Prolegomena, as translated
from the third German edition of 1894, Harnack says that in
Hatch's work " may be found the most ample proof for the
conception of the early history of dogma which is set forth in
the following pages." It would not be at all true to the facts
if one were to suggest that Hatch's standpoint has been generally
adopted by British scholars who have paid special attention to
the subject of Church History and the history of dogma. But
the view to which he gave such forcible expression has undoubtedly had a wide influence, though probably among non-Anglican
theologians rather than among Anglicans. Those who hold
that in the early centuries too close a union was effected between
the Christian religion and Greek philosophy, and that the creeds
and formularies of the Church are too much in the debt of a
Greek metaphysic which belongs (so it is often stated) to
a past age and is out of touch with modern thought, are in line
with the main argument of Hatch's Hibbert Lectures.

FROM THE PUBLICATION OF *LUX MUNDI* IN 1889 TO THE END OF THE CENTURY

FEW books in modern times have so clearly marked the presence of a new era and so deeply influenced its character as the volume of essays by a number of Oxford men which was published in the latter part of the year 1889 under the title of *Lux Mundi*. That the twelfth edition should have appeared in 1891 is itself a remarkable fact. The intense interest which it aroused was largely due to the essay contributed by the Editor, Charles Gore, at that time Principal of the Pusey House, Oxford, on the subject of " The Holy Spirit and Inspiration." That one who held a post so closely associated with the revered memory of Dr. Pusey, one, moreover, whose influence in Oxford was in line with that of the great Tractarians, Liddon, Pusey, and, half a century earlier, Newman himself, should endorse, with whatever care and reservations, those conclusions as to the Old Testament which had appeared to Pusey, and still appeared to Liddon, to be utterly incompatible with the Christian faith; that, in addition, he should refuse to allow that questions regarding the Old Testament could be settled by an appeal to words of Christ, and should affirm a doctrine of the Lord's human nature akin to that which Lutheran theologians had expressed, was a profound and most unwelcome surprise to great numbers of High Churchmen as well as to Evangelicals. Gore had made his meaning quite plain. Our Lord, he said, " willed so to restrain the beams of Deity as to observe the limits of the science of His age, and He puts Himself in the same relation to its historical knowledge." In a note he appealed to the scriptural texts, 2 Cor. viii. 9 and Phil. ii. 7, as expressing the notion of a " self-emptying " which was a " continuous act of self-sacrifice." Thus the Biblical positions which Gore had adopted both led up to and were based upon a kenotic theology which up till then had received no approval from any Anglican theologian.

But, while popular and controversial interest converged upon Gore's article, the real significance of the volume lay deeper. That is to be seen first in the sub-title of the book, " A series of studies in the religion of the Incarnation." This pointed to a change in theological emphasis, from the Atonement to the Incarnation itself. It might be going too far if one said that for the Essayists the Incarnation—that is, the taking of human nature by the Son of God—was the essential Christian Gospel: but their thought looked in that direction, and undoubtedly was influential in directing the attention of Anglican High Churchmen and of others towards the dogmatic significance of the fact that God had been made man. The writer of the essay on the Atonement, the Rev. and Hon. Arthur Lyttelton, expressed more than once his sense of the harm that had resulted from " the isolation of the truth of the Atonement from other parts of Christian doctrine ": it is probable that the other writers would all have agreed with him here. Walter Lock, afterwards Lady Margaret Professor at Oxford, and Francis Paget, who was to end his life as Bishop of Oxford, in their contributions on the Church and the Sacraments respectively, found the ultimate starting-point for the teaching which they gave in the fact of the Incarnation. Secondly, the volume was manifestly eirenical in respect of the relations between Christian doctrine and contemporary tendencies in secular thought. So far from there being any polemic against Darwinism and the theory of evolution as incompatible with Christian faith, Aubrey Moore, writing on " The Christian Doctrine of God," says outright that " Darwinism . . . under the guise of a foe, did the work of a friend. It has conferred upon philosophy and religion an inestimable benefit, by showing us that we must choose between two alternatives. Either God is everywhere present in nature or He is nowhere. He cannot be here and not there." Moreover, many of the essayists had been pupils of the famous Oxford philosopher, T. H. Green. Mark Pattison had, in his caustic way, observed that the philosopher's honey was carried off to the Tractarian hive. Green was not an orthodox Christian; his metaphysic was of the neo-Hegelian brand. The fact that these younger High Churchmen could make use of it for their own purposes witnesses to their readiness for intellectual experiment in the expression of Christian truth. They were entirely firm in their dogmatic positions, but there was a lack of rigidity in their outlook as compared with what had been customary among Churchmen.

A storm of controversy broke out as a result of *Lux Mundi*. It was realized both by Evangelicals and by High Churchmen that the essayists had abandoned the idea of the inerrancy of Holy Scripture. To none did the book come as so great a shock as to Liddon, who more than any other man carried on the tradition of Dr. Pusey. To say that *Lux Mundi* " killed " Liddon is a rhetorical underlining of its effect upon the great preacher. That it was a blow which affected his whole nature and made him less able and perhaps less concerned to resist illness is doubtless no more than the truth. It is to be noted that R. W. Church, one of the greatest of all Deans of St. Paul's, Liddon's close friend, and of all the great Tractarians the most judicious and wide-minded, did not share Liddon's views on *Lux Mundi*. Gradually the critical position as to the Old Testament which Gore had accepted won the assent of numbers of High Churchmen. There remained a group of those who would to-day be called " fundamentalists," but they exercised continually less influence, and among High Churchmen or Anglo-Catholics to-day who are men of Biblical scholarship the fundamentalist position would have no supporters.

It was round the Old Testament that the question of the Higher Criticism was turning. A work of the first importance in support of what may be called the " critical " as contrasted with the " traditional " view appeared in 1891, in *An Introduction to the Literature of the Old Testament*, by S. R. Driver, who had succeeded Pusey as Regius Professor of Hebrew at Oxford. One sentence from the Preface to the first edition will indicate Driver's position. " It is impossible," he writes, " to doubt that the main conclusions of critics with reference to the authorship of the books of the Old Testament rest upon reasonings the cogency of which cannot be denied without denying the ordinary principles by which history is judged and evidence estimated." Driver was no reckless investigator, and in so far as he was a theologian as well as a Biblical scholar he was hardly to be described as a " liberal." On the subject of our Lord's human knowledge his standpoint was essentially the same as Gore's, to whose essay he appeals in the Preface.

The *Introduction* passed through four editions in a year, and became the recognized English text-book on the literary problems of the Old Testament for those who were prepared to make the critical view their own. It gained the approbation of English and Scottish scholars who were working in the same field. The work of Robertson Smith was bearing fruit north of the Tweed in the writings of A. B. Davidson, A. R. S. Kennedy, and George Adam Smith, whose commentary upon Isaiah was to be one of the greatest of modern expository works upon the Scriptures; while in England T. K. Cheyne, who was later to become the most revolutionary of Old Testament critics, and H. E. Ryle, the son of one of the leaders of Protestant Evangelicalism, afterwards Bishop of Liverpool, expressed their approval of Driver's work. A. F. Kirkpatrick, the Cambridge scholar, was more guarded but still appreciative.

Among Anglican Evangelicals there was as yet no movement towards the critical position comparable with that which the *Lux Mundi* group had set going among High Churchmen. H. E. Ryle was not typical. H. C. G. Moule, the revered head of Ridley Hall, Cambridge, and Norrisian Professor of Divinity, who was afterwards to follow Westcott as Bishop of Durham, was strictly conservative in his outlook. Henry Wace, successor in 1903 to F. W. Farrar as Dean of Canterbury, a man of learning, intellectual ability, and much controversial acuteness, stood on the same side, as did the best-known and most forceful of the Evangelical parochial clergy, Prebendary Webb-Peploe, vicar of St. Paul's, Onslow Square, in London. The day of what is now called Liberal Evangelicalism had not yet dawned.

On the other hand, the Higher Criticism had begun to make its way among some of the leaders of English Nonconformity as well as in Scotland. R. F. Horton and A. S. Peake, two of the first Nonconformists to be elected to fellowships at Oxford Colleges, gave their support to the main lines of the critical attitude towards the Old Testament. Horton's *Inspiration and the Bible* (1888) made a stir in Nonconformist circles not unlike that which Gore's essay in *Lux Mundi* produced among Anglicans, and a year later John Clifford, who, in the controversies over education and other matters, was to become the very head and front of what was termed "political Nonconformity," was on the same side, though not an original Biblical scholar. The

conservative tradition was upheld by those who followed in
the steps of the famous preacher C. H. Spurgeon. Spurgeon
died in 1892, and before his death he had come into controversy
with Clifford and others who were prepared to accept the
critical position. Known as the " Downgrade controversy,"
from Spurgeon's attack upon theological tendencies which
seemed to him to mark a defection from the necessary standards
of Christian faith, it revealed the tension which was being felt
in Nonconformist circles, and may be compared with the
Anglican storms which broke out after *Lux Mundi*. And just
because the stability of the faith was more closely associated
with Biblical infallibility among Nonconformists than was the
case with Anglican High Churchmen, who laid stress upon the
teaching office of the Church and its authority in the sphere
of doctrine, the issues of criticism were more nearly related,
among the former, to controversies of a directly theological
character.

It may be noted that as yet the New Testament had not become
the subject of sharp contention. That was to come, but for
more reasons than one the storm which had burst in respect of
critical theories about the Old Testament was threatening the
peace of New Testament study. For many years, from about
the middle of the 90's onwards, the most influential figure in
the world of English New Testament scholarship was William
Sanday, the Lady Margaret Professor at Oxford. As a savant he
was not inferior to the great scholars of Germany of whose works
he was a diligent student. He was no supporter of the theory
of Biblical inerrancy, as his Bampton Lectures on Inspiration
made clear. But he was cautious, sympathetic to older views,
and during these years of much the same theological mind as
his colleague in the chair of Hebrew, Professor Driver. In particular, till quite late in his life his attitude to the miraculous
element in the Gospels was consonant with a conservative
rather than with a radical theology. Where he definitely advanced
upon the great Cambridge scholars was in his readiness to learn
from German scholarship. He was far more of a cosmopolitan
student than either Westcott or Hort. That he did to some
extent sacrifice his independence, and pay too much deference
to views of a German origin, is possibly the case, though, at
the same time, his power of detachment ought not to be over-

looked: what is certain is that he brought to the study of the New Testament, and especially of the Gospels, a sanity and a wise judgment which were of very great value at a time when the relations between English and German scholarship were becoming increasingly intimate.

But towards the end of the century the field of religious and theological discussion in England was dominated by the outbreak of violent controversy concerning the ritual and ceremonial tendencies of a large number of the clergy of the Church of England. For some three or four years England rang with attacks upon the advanced High Church clergy, while they and their lay supporters were not backward in defence. The Press and Parliament gave an attention to the matter which showed how deeply feelings were stirred, and the phrase " The Crisis in the Church " passed into common parlance. This is not the place for a history of the controversy. Its importance for the student of religious movements in England lies in the fact that during these years, and probably for the last time, an attempt was made to control by legal action the High Church movement. The attempt failed. The Bishops, though many or most of them had little sympathy with what was often described as " ritualism," were not prepared to take or approve action which, had it succeeded, would have meant the driving out of the Church of England of some of the most hard-working and self-sacrificing of its clergy. But, more than that, they realized that any such campaign would have resulted in all who felt themselves to be the heirs of the Tractarian revival ranging themselves with the " ritualists," even though they might disapprove of not a little which the " ritualists " both did and taught. The attack, therefore, was left without any real official support. Even so it was for a time very formidable, and had the sympathy of the great majority of members of the House of Commons. But it could not gain its final objectives, and it gradually diminished in strength.

But it is interesting to note that there is continuity between this embittered controversy and the events of 1927 and 1928, when the House of Commons twice refused its assent to the proposals as to Prayer Book revision for which legal sanction was sought. For this revision took its rise in the findings of the Royal Commission on Ecclesiastical Disorders, which was appointed in 1904 and made its report in 1906. If the Evangelical and Protestant party had failed to secure decisive action against the advanced High Churchmen in the early years of the century, it could nevertheless claim that it had prevented the legalization of changes in the Book of Common Prayer which would have given direct sanction to High Church teaching and ceremonies. At the same time it should be noted that in 1927 and 1928 a number of the most convinced Anglo-Catholics, as they had now come to be called, were strongly opposed to the contemplated changes. Some of these changes seemed to them to go much too far in a modernist direction, while, in respect of the Holy Communion, the proposed revision diverged from that western liturgical tradition which they specially revered.

CHAPTER II

FROM THE BEGINNING OF THE TWENTIETH CENTURY TO THE
OUTBREAK OF THE GREAT WAR

THE attack upon " Ritualism " in the Church of England
was a challenge to the whole Tractarian point of view.
The Tractarians had not been all at one in their attitude
to the Reformation; what they had insisted on was the continuity of the post-Reformation Church with the Church of
primitive times in respect of doctrine, and especially of sacramental doctrine, since that was where controversy was acute.
They claimed that as English Churchmen they were free to
teach the doctrine of the Real Presence, the Eucharistic Sacrifice,
the Apostolic Succession, the Priesthood—not least with regard
to Absolution, Prayers for the dead, and so on. Most of those
who claimed descent from the Tractarians would have stoutly
denied that in giving this teaching they were, in the parlance
of the day, " Romanizing." There had always been an inclination
on the part of some of those associated with the Tractarian
Movement to minimize differences between the Church of
England and the Church of Rome, and even to find in the Church
of Rome the ideal towards which the Church of England should
look. Hurrell Froude was becoming of this mind in the later
years of his life, and W. G. Ward, before he went over, had
expressed this point of view in his book, *The Ideal of a Christian
Church*. But it had not been the position of Keble, nor of
Newman, till his faith in the Church of England began to be
shaken; while Pusey, though he looked for agreements rather
than disagreements between the Church of England and the
Church of Rome, was never disturbed in his belief that the
Church of England was doctrinally in accord with the primitive
Church, and that that fact, along with the retention of the
historic ministry, gave the Church of England all the authority
that it needed. The *Lux Mundi* group was substantially of the
same mind, and the result of the years of controversy was, on
the whole, to consolidate the High Church party. In regard to
theological equipment, a party which could count such men as

Charles Gore, Henry Scott Holland, R. C. Moberly, and J. R. Illingworth as of its number had no cause to fear for the presentation of its case.

A special word must be said about R. C. Moberly, since two of his books were of very great significance. His *Ministerial Priesthood* (1897) challenged the great Lightfoot, whose famous essay, *The Christian Ministry*, had been regarded as the vindication of the unsacerdotal character of the ministry in the primitive Church. Moberly made no claim to an equality with Lightfoot on purely historical matters; but he contended that in the theological sphere Lightfoot was open to the charge of taking for granted certain hypotheses and postulates, which coloured the whole of the famous essay, while they were in point of fact open to grave objection. Two of these assumptions may be quoted in order to make the lines of Moberly's disagreement with Lightfoot clear. To the " unconscious substructure " of the essay belonged the postulate that " the literal and real meaning of the words sacrifice and priesthood is that which they bore in the Old Testament: by this all other applications of the words must be measured and judged. Again: If ministry is representative of the Body as a whole, then the Body as a whole, and every member thereof, must implicitly possess the right to minister." Moberly's own view rested on a conception of the relation between Christ and the Church, between the inward and the outward, between the ministry and the laity, to which he believed that neither Roman Catholic doctrine, nor Protestant conceptions, nor Bishop Lightfoot did justice.

Ministerial Priesthood is not so remarkable a book as *Atonement and Personality* (1901), but it is probable that the influence it has exercised has been much greater. The later volume was certainly one of the most impressive theological works of its age. It was, indeed, a study in systematic theology such as had not been produced for many years from within the Church of England. Nor must its importance as a contribution to the doctrine of the Atonement be minimized. Moberly took his stand with the classical soteriology of the Church in its stress upon an " objective " act of atonement made by Christ in His death. But it was his conviction that there had been a wrong tendency to isolate Calvary and not to bring the atoning death into a true relation with the work of the Holy Spirit and the life of the

Church. The absence of any reference to the Holy Spirit Moberly regarded as the gravest defect in the famous work of Dr. Dale, *The Atonement*. Accordingly he saw in Dale's work a one-sidedness which, with all the merits of the book, merits which Moberly fully recognized, meant the presence in it of "something really retrograde." In particular, Moberly was critical of the emphasis laid by Dale on the notion of penal suffering in the Cross, where Dale held that Christ submitted to the "actual penalty of sin." He himself put forward in a more elaborate form an idea which had already been expounded by McLeod Campbell in his treatise, *The Nature of the Atonement* (1856). McLeod Campbell had thought of Christ as making in the name of humanity the perfect confession of sin before God. "This confession," he wrote in a famous phrase, "as to its own nature must have been *a perfect Amen in humanity to the judgment of God on the sin of man*." Moberly, starting from an analysis of the conceptions of punishment, penitence, and forgiveness, and laying great stress on the self-identification of Christ with humanity, worked out his notion of Christ as the perfect Penitent, the One who, just because He was Himself without sin, was able to express the full reality of penitence. It is by this notion that Moberly's distinctive contribution to soteriology stands or falls, and it cannot be said that it has made for itself an abiding place among the many theories which have gathered round the fundamental faith in Christ as the Mediator and in His atoning work.

The High Church party gained immensely on the theological side from the fact of the intellectual coherence of its various positions, and of the general agreement on all the great questions of its best-known representatives. It is true that an equally large measure of unity was true of the Evangelical leaders. Men like Moule, Dimock, Drury, Girdlestone, and Wace (though Wace is hardly to be ranked as an Evangelical *pur sang*) were theologians faithful to a tradition which they expounded with ample learning and ability. The Anglican Evangelicals have had a far more distinguished record in theology than is apt to be recognized. But their influence on the general thought of the Church suffered from, among other causes, their attitude on the subject of the Bible and their inattention to the problems arising in connexion with the philosophy of religion. They were far more rigid in the face of the results which were claimed to follow from the methods of the Higher Criticism than were those High Churchmen who followed in the steps of Gore and the *Lux Mundi* school, while they made no effort to construct a Christian philosophy of religion, which could appeal on purely intellectual grounds to minds conversant with modern movements in science and metaphysics. It is, of course, possible to hold that in both these respects the Evangelical theologians were in the right; but it can hardly be doubted that their doctrinal appeal was lessened owing to what seemed to many to be a narrowness in their outlook.

Contributions similar to *Lux Mundi*, in being the result of the co-operation of a number of scholars, made their appearance in the early years of the twentieth century. In 1902 a group of Oxford tutors produced the volume to which they assigned the name *Contentio Veritatis*; and in 1905 a larger number of Cambridge scholars issued the *Cambridge Theological Essays*, which was followed in 1909 by the *Cambridge Biblical Essays*. No one of these, nor of other joint works, had the influence or aroused the controversy which had followed upon the publication of *Lux Mundi*, or, nearly half a century earlier, of *Essays and Reviews*. This was partly due, in the case of the Cambridge books, to the greater individualism of Cambridge theological tendencies as compared with that of Oxford. It is true that the association between the great Cambridge Three had been as close as any bond that had united Oxford scholars; but Cambridge was not the home of movements directed towards a particular end. Such was not and never had been its native genius. Moreover, there was no such intensive influence upon Church life as a whole flowing out of Cambridge as was characteristic of Oxford. *Contentio Veritatis* was of more importance. It was neither a theological nor an ecclesiatical manifesto, but it called attention to the presence in Oxford of scholars who could be classed neither as High Churchmen nor as Evangelicals, while their standpoint was not that of such a representative of the older Broad Churchmanship as Benjamin Jowett, the famous Master of Balliol.

On the personal side the volume has the interest that it gave further evidence of the rising importance, as a philosophical theologian singularly independent in his judgments, of W. R.

Inge. His Bampton Lectures of 1899 on the subject of Christian Mysticism had awakened or reawakened interest in a field of Christian thought and experience which lay apart from the main routes of theological discussion and, still more, of ecclesiastical controversies. And if in this respect a great change has taken place, so that mysticism and religious experience in general have become familiar themes and passed into the forefront of religious attention and theological enquiry, that is probably due to Dr. Inge more than to any other English thinker and writer, with the one exception of William James, whose classic work, *The Varieties of Relgious Experience*, was published some three years later than Inge's Bampton Lectures. In *Contentio Veritatis* Inge dealt with the doctrine of the Person of Christ and with the sacraments. To the part he has played in discussions on the former subject it will be necessary to refer later on in connexion with various writings and debates which centred in one or other aspect of the Christological theme.

With regard to sacraments and other matters which need to be considered in relation to the doctrine of the Church, Dr. Inge has had little to contribute. The sense of a near kinship between mysticism and sacramentalism which some theologians would possess has been in no way prominent in the writings of Dr. Inge. His strong protest against the Ritschlian notion of mysticism as pre-eminently belonging to the Catholic type of piety, to be found in his Paddock Lectures on *Personal Idealism and Mysticism* published in 1907, could hardly have been made quite in its actual form if he had allowed for a true inner relation between mystical and sacramental piety. But for him mysticism was describable as " a type of religion which puts the inner light above human authority and finds its sacraments everywhere." Into the rights and wrongs of the position which Dr. Inge adopted, from which, so far as I know, he has never withdrawn, it is no purpose of this volume to enter. But it may be noted that on the general question of the relation of mysticism to Christianity and Christian piety the sharpest differences would be found among theologians of the first rank. A round-table discussion on the question, if one imagines such men as W. R. Inge, Wilhelm Herrmann, Friedrich von Hügel, and Emil Brunner as seated at it, would have been of an interest, and, indeed, of an excitement, such as one could hardly exaggerate:

but it is very doubtful whether there would have been more unity at the end than at the beginning.

In the first years of the new century there was no special tension in the field of theological as distinguished from ecclesiastical debate. This state of things was soon to be changed through the pressure of New Testament problems. Questions as to the character and reliability of the Gospels, the supernatural element in Christianity, and the doctrine of the Person of Christ, came to the front. In them the final issues of the nature and truth of Christianity were involved, and far more really than in the *Lux Mundi* controversies the matters of theological debate were of vital concern to the Church. The Church of England, the Roman Catholic Church, and the English Free Churches were all in different ways faced with a critical situation, whereof the main features must now be described.

We must go back to the English edition of Harnack's lectures translated under the title of *What is Christianity?* for the starting-point. This appeared in 1901, and was recognized as the ablest statement, at once scholarly and popular, of the Liberal Protestant interpretation of Christianity that was to be found. Harnack was no radical in New Testament criticism: his later works on St. Luke and on the Acts were to prove a powerful argument in favour of the traditional authorship and the general accuracy (though Harnack rejected the definitely supernatural narratives) of the third Gospel and the book of Acts. Nor was Harnack theologically as revolutionary as was often supposed. He recognized the mystery inherent in the Person of Christ. But it is true to say that in his lectures he refused to accept the historic account of the Person of Christ as given in the doctrines of His divinity and incarnation. His deep reverence for Jesus as the supreme Teacher and the Revealer of God did not lead him to the acceptance of the Pauline and Johannine Christology and to the affirmations of the Nicene Creed. His book was widely read, and there was much in it that others besides theological Liberals could welcome, but the breach with Catholic theology was too clear and too deep for it to be very influential. It called forth replies from English scholars, among them W. Sanday, the Lady Margaret Professor at Oxford, whose authority in the study of the New Testament was during the early years of the century at its height.

But far the most remarkable reply to Harnack came from a French Roman Catholic scholar, who was already known in theological circles for his works on the text and canon of the Biblical writings. The Abbé Loisy published in 1902 a volume entitled *L'Évangile et L'Église*, to which in the second edition of 1903 he added a chapter on the Gospel sources. If any theological work of our time justifies the description " sensational," that adjective may be applied to Loisy's reply to Harnack. Its object was to justify the historic faith and theology of the (Roman) Catholic Church, but the manner in which Loisy set out to do this seemed to many besides Roman Catholic Bishops and Roman Catholic theologians to involve an apologetic and a dogmatic which could not possibly be reconciled with traditional Christian beliefs about the Gospels, about the historical Person of Jesus, and about the nature of Christian theology. The value of the Gospels (not only the fourth Gospel) as trustworthy records was greatly diminished: how greatly was to become more obvious when some years later Loisy produced his large work on the synoptic Gospels; the Christ of the Church's faith appeared to have so little in common with the Jesus of history that the phrase " comme deux Christs " was a true expression of the relation or lack of relation between Jesus and Christ; and the theology of the Church was an interpretation that met the needs of the Church's life, and safeguarded under very different forms and in very different circumstances the teaching that Jesus gave, in particular His Gospel of the Kingdom of Heaven.

L'Évangile et L'Église may be taken as the beginning of the movement which is properly described as the Modernist Movement. " Modernism " has come to be one of those terms which are used in a wide and ill-defined sense, and in England it has been employed as a variant, more comprehensive and appealing, of the old-fashioned " Broad Church." It is likely that to-day the Bishop of Birmingham (Dr. Barnes) would be regarded as the most obvious representative of Modernism. But really there are few to whom the title is less appropriate if the historical provenance of the word be considered. For Modernism was a movement within the Roman Catholic Church, and while its protagonists, Loisy among others, were anxious to come to terms with what they believed to be the results of scientific enquiry and of the historical criticism of the Bible, they were as much concerned to show that the true *ethos* of Christianity was to be found in the Roman Catholic Church, that the true development from the first Christian age onwards was that which had culminated in the great fabric of theological, institutional, and sacramental Catholicism, and that Protestantism was emphatically not a return to primitive Christianity or a recovery of its spirit.

With the fortunes of the Modernist Movement we are not here concerned, except in so far as it reacted on the theological situation in England. The reply of Loisy to Harnack raised questions with which theologians of different Christian communions were profoundly concerned. These were felt specially keenly within Anglicanism, and sharp differences revealed themselves among scholars of repute. W. R. Inge took up a position in the strongest opposition to that of Loisy. In the field of Gospel criticism his whole inclination was towards that estimate of Christ as supreme moral Teacher, wherein Harnack and the German Liberals saw so much of the outstanding grandeur and value of the Person of Jesus. On this Loisy laid no stress at all; in his work the " eschatological " understanding of the preaching of Jesus, namely the view that the Kingdom, as Jesus proclaimed it, had nothing to do with moral or social progress in this world, but was a future supernatural reality to be brought in by a catastrophic act of God, came to the front. Dr. Inge did not agree with Harnack in his attitude towards the doctrine of the Person of Christ. That in Jesus the divine Logos was incarnate has always been the most firmly held conviction of the English theologian. But one may say that of the truth of that doctrine he has always seen striking verification in the moral teaching to which the Gospels bear witness and in the life and character of the historical Jesus. But it was not only in respect of its attitude to the historical Person, but also because of what seemed to him to be the radically wrong oppositions which it set up between fact and faith, between historical and theological truth, that Dr. Inge repudiated the distinctively modernistic position. When the crisis in the Roman Church reached its final stage, he held, as he was afterwards to write in his *Confessio Fidei*, printed in the second volume of his *Outspoken Essays*, that " the Roman Church was quite right in condemning both Loisy and Tyrrell."

Inge's view of the matter was not taken by all Anglican theologians. T. A. Lacey, one of the most learned and acute theologians in the ranks of the High Churchmen, and A. L. Lilley, who had personal acquaintance with a number of the modernist leaders, were sympathetically disposed to the new movement. There was a certain temptation among those who represented the High Church tradition to adopt a kindly and generous attitude towards men who had taken the field against the Liberal Protestantism which made so sharp a division between the New Testament and the Catholic Church, and, within the New Testament, concentrated upon the moral aspects of primitive Christianity at the expense of its theological, institutional, and sacramental characteristics. Moreover, the Modernist Movement was attracting and gaining, in a general way, the support of one who had been exercising an influence that has met with considerable response from within the Church of England. George Tyrrell, while a member of the Society of Jesus, had come into prominence through writings in which he expounded the nature of Catholicism, and treated of problems that were concerned with the essence of religion and its relation to life. As he grew more and more dissatisfied with the scholastic method in theology and with certain aspects of life within the Roman Catholic Church, his own teaching came increasingly under the influence of Loisy on the Biblical side, and of some of the more philosophical modernists in the interpretation of doctrine and in what may broadly be called the philosophy of religion. His later works were definitely polemical; he had no leaning towards Protestantism, though he once lamented that he had ever left the Church of England. But his appeal was from Catholicism as he viewed it within the Church of Rome to a Catholicism that should be free from those restrictions against which he protested. When the Papal condemnations of Modernism were issued in the Decree *Lamentabili* and the Encyclical *Pascendi Gregis* in the year 1907, Tyrrell publicly criticized them; and with his own condemnation his life in communion with the Church of Rome came to an end.

The Modernist controversy had raised the whole question of the nature of primitive Christianity, and of the origins of the Christian movement in its relation to the Gospel and Person of Jesus. It was not, of course, a new question. Scholars conversant with the Biblical and theological discussions so characteristic of Germany were well aware of the ferment of ideas and conjectures, to which the *Gelehrte* of that country made each his own contribution. Particularly did Dr. Sanday keep a careful eye upon German scholarship, so much so that Mr., now Monsignor, Ronald Knox compared him to a meteorologist making his regular weather reports. In *The Life of Christ in Recent Research* which was published in 1907, and in *Christologies Ancient and Modern*, a book of three years later, Dr. Sanday examined the work that was being done in connexion with the Gospels and various types of Christological doctrine. In the latter he put forward his own suggestion, which caused much interest and discussion at the time, but has not had any permanent influence, that " the subliminal consciousness is the proper seat or *locus* of the Deity of the incarnate Christ." Dr. Sanday was a great Biblical scholar and a most valuable commentator upon the doctrinal positions, as well as the New Testament researches and interpretations, of other scholars. But he was not himself an expert dogmatic theologian, nor was he a trained philosopher, and he was apt to be carried away by too generous enthusiasms, and to be over ready to give his assent, where a better qualified and more cautious thinker would have at least reserved judgment. I would not say that in the chapters on Dr. Du Bose in the earlier volume mentioned above he overpraised the American theologian, but he did write as though Du Bose had settled a long-standing controversy in connexion with the doctrine of the Atonement, not only for Dr. Sanday himself, but more generally. Similarly, he was almost impetuous in the way in which he laid hold of the psychological theory of the subliminal consciousness, and made it the groundwork of a Christological theory.

To return to the Biblical and historical problem, while the ebb and flow of criticism and discussion in Germany was known to British scholars, and was to some extent passed on by them, it was some time before anything happened to arouse keen interest and concern in circles which paid no particular attention to the debates of the experts. This state of things was affected and even radically changed by certain books or articles, which were the cause of sharp and sometimes bitter controversy and led to great unsettlement. To focus attention on these writings is perhaps as simple a way as is possible for the appreciation of theological movements during this period.

The first of these books to appear was *The New Theology* (1907), the work of the Rev. R. J. Campbell, who some years before had succeeded the famous preacher Joseph Parker as Minister of the City Temple. Mr. Campbell had come over to Congregationalism from Anglicanism, but it would not be unfair to say that to his natural *ethos* or habit of mind the theological tradition characteristic of English Nonconformity was never congenial. In particular, the substitutionary or penal conception of the Atonement, as that was, with whatever reservations, expounded and passionately defended by Dr. James Denney, one of the most powerful of Scottish New Testament theologians, and by Dr. P. T. Forsyth, himself a Congregationalist and Principal of Hackney College in London, was alien to Mr. Campbell. But his book went far beyond any restatement of one doctrine. It was a reinterpretation of Christian theology under the influence of the idea of divine immanence. Especially did it appear as though the Incarnation itself were regarded by the author as no more than the supreme example of God's indwelling, and the distinction between God and man were obliterated through a comprehensive Pantheism. If this theology were to be accepted as not only new but also true, it was obvious that the theological tradition of the English Free Churches was gravely defective at its central points, both where it shared the historic beliefs as to God and Christ which the Catholic creeds expressed, and where it emphasized doctrines of the sixteenth-century Reformers. Mr. Campbell had his defenders, but the weight of Free Church opinion was decisively against him. The most learned and influential of Free Church theologians, Dr. A. M. Fairbairn, Principal of Mansfield College, Oxford, was no less severe in his judgments than was Dr. Forsyth; while the greatest of English Nonconformist journals, *The British Weekly*, brilliantly edited by Dr. Robertson Nicoll, was in sharp opposition. It is not necessary to discuss how far Mr. Campbell was misunderstood, and the real extent of his variation from the New Testament teaching and from the creed that Catholics and Evangelicals held in common. In course of time Mr. Campbell himself made it clear that he no longer held, if he had ever held, the doctrines supposed to be fundamental in the New Theology, and re-found his true spiritual home in the Church of England, of which he is still a distinguished minister, Canon, and till lately Chancellor, of Chichester.

Nothing in Mr. Campbell's exposition of the New Theology gave greater offence than his apparent refusal to allow that Jesus was divine in any other way than was possible for every man, however much it was true that the harmony of the divine and the human was perfect in Jesus beyond what had ever come to pass in any other man. Hence the title " Christ " or " The Christ " could be regarded as not the possession of Jesus only, but as potential in the case of any man who was realizing the best possibilities of human nature. Mr. Campbell himself in an article of the year 1909 wrote: " His Christhood would be of little avail if it did not awaken ours; Christhood is manhood at its highest power."

With this in mind we may pass to the second volume, which during this time was of special significance and in which Mr. Campbell wrote the sentence just quoted. In the year 1909, a Congregationalist minister, the Rev. R. Roberts of Bradford, contributed to the well-known quarterly, *The Hibbert Journal*, an article entitled " Jesus or Christ ?". The gist of the article, which was concerned with the Person of Jesus, as He is presented in the synoptic Gospels, and with interpretations given by modern theologians, may be found in a sentence close to the end: " Identifying Jesus with Christ, they make God a Being who is omnipotent, yet limited in power; omniscient, yet defective in knowledge; infinitely good, yet One who declines ' to turn any part of His knowledge as God into science for man.' " And that seemed to Mr. Roberts to be " flat contradiction." The article led to a discussion that passed outside the limits of academical debate, and in the same year a supplement to the *Hibbert Journal* was published with the title, *Jesus or Christ ?*, to which various eminent scholars, theologians, and Church-leaders, British and foreign, contributed. As the writers represented exceedingly different points of view, it cannot be said that the volume had the character and effect of a summing-up and a settlement. But it did help to make clear the fact that can never be forgotten without disastrous consequences for rational argument, be the conclusions of such argument what they may, that the question, *in supereminenti sensu* Christian, is the

question, " What think ye of Christ ? " If " Christ " is really
a generic term, in such manner that we all are or may come to
be " Christs," the fact that Jesus is called Christ, and that we
speak of Jesus Christ, need not be of any ultimate significance.
In that case, the religion of the New Testament, its substance,
not merely its form, can never be ours in the way in which it
was the religion of former generations of Christians.

Neither *The New Theology* nor *Jesus or Christ ?* is, as a book, of
lasting importance. It is otherwise with the third volume,
which serves as a kind of signpost of theological movement
during this period. In 1910 Albert Schweitzer's New Testament
study, *Von Reimarus zu Wrede*, appeared in an English translation
under the title of *The Quest of the Historical Jesus*, and was com-
mended in an important preface contributed by Professor
F. C. Burkitt, the Norrisian Professor at Cambridge and one
of the most learned and versatile of New Testament scholars.
His book, *The Gospel History and its Transmission* (1906), had
been of high importance for its examination of the literary
and historical problems which arise out of the synoptic Gospels.
As to Schweitzer's work, it is not too much to say that for a
quarter of a century New Testament study in England has been
continually concerned with the interpretation that he gave of
the Kingdom of God in the preaching of Jesus.

Without doubt Schweitzer made it very difficult to identify
the Kingdom, according to its meaning in the Gospels, with
moral and social progress in this world. To all those Liberal
Christians who believed that they rightly understood Jesus
when they thought of the Kingdom as coming by an immanental
process and destined to permeate the life of the present world,
Schweitzer's " consistent eschatology," his interpretation of
the Kingdom as having nothing to do with man's efforts but
wholly dependent upon God's decision to bring it in by an
apocalyptic and catastrophic act, was a deadly menace. The
whole conception of Jesus as the supreme moral Teacher,
who had enunciated the laws of the good life, was, if Schweitzer
was right, completely off the lines of the Gospels. But it was
not only the Liberals who were threatened in their deepest
convictions. Those who, in accordance with the age-long
Christian tradition, saw in the Figure of Jesus in the Gospels
the divine Son of God had to consider how they stood in relation

to an interpretation which insisted that if the Gospel story could be trusted at all, it was the story of One who believed that the Kingdom was about to be established by supernatural intervention. When it did not come as soon as He anticipated, He deliberately sought His own death, in the belief that His death, the death of Him who was to be manifested as the Messiah, would be accepted by God as an atonement for sin, and thereby hasten the coming of the Kingdom. So He went to Jerusalem to die, and did die: but the Kingdom did not come.

Now, Schweitzer's reconstruction was in line with the orthodox reading of the Gospel story in so far as it attached great importance to the Cross. The idea that the Cross had no special dogmatic importance and that St. Paul had been responsible for the stress laid upon the death of Christ, was repudiated by Schweitzer no less than by the mass of English and Scottish Biblical scholars. But if the whole substance of the Gospel, as Jesus had proclaimed it, was eschatology, and if His hopes and anticipations had not been fulfilled, the most serious questions arose as to the abiding value for mankind of His Gospel and of His Person. The same sort of issue was raised as had appeared in connexion with Loisy and Tyrrell, and in a manner easier to appreciate. A remark once made by T. R. Glover, well known at Cambridge both as a classical scholar and as a leading Free Churchman (Baptist), to the effect that on Schweitzer's theory it was difficult to see in what way Jesus of Nazareth differed from a fanatic like Bar-Cochba, was, anyhow at that time, a fair statement of the gravity of the issues raised. No immediate solution was found. But British scholarship is always likely to recoil before the sharp *entweder-oder* of German dialectic. For Schweitzer the choice was one between thorough-going eschatology and thorough-going scepticism, such as he connected particularly with W. Wrede, Professor at Breslau. In England such a choice was impossible. That Schweitzer and the eschatological interpretation have influenced English work upon the Gospels is certainly the case. The old Liberal notion of the Kingdom is never likely to be revived. But that the Gospel which Jesus preached was pure eschatology— that has not won the adherence of scholars here. And on the doctrinal point it is doubtful whether any new matter of principle had come up for consideration over and above what, since *Lux Mundi*, a number of theologians had been prepared to recognize in relation to the conditions of the Incarnation.

Already in his Congregational Union Lecture of 1909 on *The Person and Place of Jesus Christ*, which was to become his greatest work, P. T. Forsyth had argued strongly against the idea that in the Incarnation Christ must still have been omniscient and omnipotent, and found no difficulty at all in admitting the presence in Christ of " those errors, in respect of the form of the future no less than the history of the past, which he shared with his time and race." More cautiously, but along the same line of full recognition of the limitations involved in a true incarnation, was von Hügel to write in his paper on " The Apocalyptic Element in the Teaching of Jesus " (1919), now published in the first volume of his *Essays and Addresses on the Philosophy of Religion*. Jesus " could not but imagine, think, feel and will the deepest truths and facts of His mission with Jewish categories, images, emotions ": and if He "held that the world's present order would be terminated by an act of God, He could not image and propound this act other than as sudden and rapid." It is likely that a Roman Catholic theologian would not allow the truth of this sentence precisely as von Hügel wrote it, and he certainly would not admit the conclusions that von Hügel would most probably have drawn; nor would an Evangelical theologian, for whom Biblical inerrancy and the infallibility of Jesus Christ are to be asserted without any reservation whatever and in relation to every class of subject. But there would be very wide agreement among Anglican and Free Church theologians that a whole-hearted acceptance of the Catholic doctrine of the Person of Christ does not involve any one particular attitude towards the eschatological passages in the Gospels.

As to the eschatological problem itself, it is interesting to note that in a quite recent volume on *The Doctrine of the Work of Christ* (1937) Dr. Cave, who succeeded Dr. Garvie as Principal of New College, London, writes that " the ' eschatological ' controversy seems at last to be drawing to a close. . . . More recent scholarship provides an interpretation of the Kingdom which makes it possible for one aspect of our Lord's teaching to be recognized without the other being ignored." He has in mind the work of, among others, Dr. T. W. Manson and Professor C. H. Dodd, who refuse the old contrast " present or future," and emphasize the fact that in the Gospels the Kingdom, which man certainly cannot bring in, is already present in the Person and activity of Jesus. One may note that a fresh orientation towards the Gospels is given in the work of the late Sir Edwyn Hoskyns and Mr. Noel Davey, who in *The Riddle of the New Testament* (1931) have paid special attention to the relation in which material in the synoptic Gospels and, in particular, the Messianic question stands to the Old Testament. The study of the Gospels can never be a pure science, but there is such a thing as a scientific attitude towards it; and it may be claimed for English scholars of this century that they have given valuable assistance in the effort to reach it.

The controversy as to the new theology, which had started with Mr. Campbell's book of that name, had affected mainly the English Free Churches. The controversy as to the miraculous element in Christianity, which arose out of the volume entitled *Miracles in the New Testament* (1911), by the Rev. J. M. Thompson, Dean of Divinity at Magdalen College, Oxford, was carried on chiefly by scholars of the Church of England. It was indeed a matter in which the position of all Christians was involved. But the urgency of the issue was felt the more acutely within the Church of England because of the place of the Creeds in the faith and worship of that Church. Mr. Thompson in his book argued that the events recorded in the Gospels as miracles had not, in their original historical setting, been miracles. That Christ had performed remarkable cures he did not deny, but these were not miracles in the sense that no natural explanation could be given of them. But that Christ walked on the sea, or fed thousands of people with a few loaves and fishes, or raised men from the dead, he did deny. And, in particular, he denied that Christ had been born of a Virgin and that He had risen *in His body* from the grave. With the course and value of his argument we are not concerned. His book is almost entirely a consideration of the New Testament evidence. He maintained that his conclusions did not involve any denial of the Christian faith that in Jesus Christ God is incarnate.

Mr. Thompson had had his predecessors. Dr. Gore when Bishop of Worcester had dealt with the case of Mr. Beeby, who had denied the truth of the Virgin Birth. The very learned, if, in his later days, very erratic, Old Testament scholar, Professor

T. K. Cheyne, had published a work which had the effect of
reducing the miraculous side of the New Testament to mythology.
But Mr. Thompson's book created a far greater stir. Its challenging and uncompromising character; the position occupied by
its author; the fact that his traditions were High rather than
Broad Church; to which may be added a general sensitiveness
at that time on whatever was closely concerned with the historical nature of the New Testament and with the doctrine of the
Person of Christ—all contributed to bring the book into the
forefront of attention and to make it the starting-point for a
prolonged theological debate. With the disciplinary aspects of
the matter, and with the consequences that followed in relation
to Mr. Thompson's position at Magdalen College, we are not
concerned. What it is important to realize is that the controversy
about miracle could not be isolated. It broadened out into
discussions that ranged round the nature of God's self-revelation,
the authority and interpretation of the Creeds, and the meaning
and implications of the Incarnation.

To those discussions many of the foremost theologians of
the Church of England contributed in various ways. It was not
simply a question of agreeing or disagreeing with Mr. Thompson.
There was the further question of how far he had the right as
a minister of the Church of England to put forward views which
were certainly inconsistent with the letter of the Creeds.
Something like a pamphlet war was seen. Dr. Gore, the Bishop
of Oxford, was the most notable figure on the one side. Neither
then nor at any other time did he allow that it was legitimate to
take the clauses in the Creed which referred to our Lord's
birth and resurrection in any other than their obvious meaning.
On the other side stood Dr. Bethune-Baker, the Lady Margaret
Professor at Cambridge, an expert theologian in the region of
the history of Christian doctrine, who had come, or was coming,
to conclusions as to the miraculous element in Christianity not
dissimilar from that of Mr. Thompson. His colleague, Professor
Gwatkin, a learned and brilliant Church historian, though not
himself in agreement with Mr. Thompson, criticized Dr. Gore
for what he held to be Gore's error in according to the Creeds an
authority of a kind that he refused to the Bible. It may be noted
that throughout this controversy, and whenever like issues came
up, for instance in the case of Dr. Hensley Henson who was

appointed to be Bishop of Hereford in 1918, those who were in opposition to Gore made much of what they regarded as his inconsistency, in that he accepted critical conclusions incompatible with any doctrine of Biblical inerrancy, while he refused to allow any analogous criticism of clauses in the Creeds. For Gore the two matters were not *in pari passu*. For him, belief in the Lord's virginal birth and bodily resurrection was part of the historic faith of Christendom, integrally bound up with faith in Christ as God incarnate, and such a belief could not be turned into an open question. Clearly it was a case of different presuppositions being in control.

But in the whole series of pamphlets it is probable that none caused such a stir as Dr. Sanday's intervention under the title of *Bishop Gore's Challenge to Criticism*, which he published in 1914. Dr. Sanday had not formally declared himself till then; a sermon before the University of Cambridge in 1912 was rather a criticism than a support of Mr. Thompson. But even in 1912 he was moving away from that cautious acceptance of miracle in the life of Jesus which had characterized his earlier writings, in particular his *Outlines of the Life of Christ*, the reprint of a famous article in Hastings' Dictionary of the Bible. In his answer to Gore he definitely, though once more with his habitual restraint of statement, made it clear that he did not think of our Lord's birth and resurrection as miraculous events according to the usual interpretation of the phrase. Yet then and always he was insistent on his full belief in what, as distinguished from the miraculous, may be called the supernatural element in those events. He did not dogmatically deny: but, as to the birth of Christ, where the issue is perhaps specially manifest, he was inclined not to accept the particular miracle as it stands in the first and third Gospels, but to be content with the belief that the birth was in the fullest way sanctified; it was in all its circumstances a holy event. So in a series of discussions with Dr. T. B. Strong, then Dean of Christ Church, Oxford, and privately circulated in 1916, he wrote: "I have said that I believe fully in a supernatural birth; I believe fully in a birth that was surrounded with every circumstance of sanctity." And one may sum up his position by saying that he was more concerned to defend the right of Mr. Thompson and others to state their position, without being subject to

censure as though they were doing something they had no right
to do, than to deny the presence of miracle in the life of Christ.

Not wholly unrelated to this controversy on miracle, though
in no sense the product of it, was the publication in 1912 by
seven Oxford men of the book *Foundations*. Its sub-title was
" A Statement of Christian Belief in Terms of Modern Thought."
It was a book of considerable importance. Like *Lux Mundi* and
Contentio Veritatis it was the work of men of academic reputation;
but the average age of the contributors was considerably lower
than in the case of the earlier volumes. Its unity was one of general outlook rather than of exact theological, still less of ecclesiastical, agreement. It had to some extent the character of an
apologia for the truth of Christianity, but readers of conservative
views were likely to feel that with the defence went more of
a re-statement of Christian belief than they could easily assimilate.
Thus B. H. Streeter in his article on " The Historic Christ,"
while holding firmly to the reality of resurrection appearances
of Christ, was inclined, speaking for himself and not for all
(was he for any ?) of his colleagues, not to accept the Gospel
story of the Empty Tomb.

W. Temple in his article on " The Divinity of Christ "
showed himself critical of the categories employed in the
building up of the Patristic Christology. " The formula of
Chalcedon," he wrote, " is in fact a confession of the bank-
ruptcy of Greek Patristic Theology." This sentence, with which
may be associated another, " the chief result of Greek theology
so far was to show (not indeed to contemporaries) the impossibility of a theology in terms of substance," has often been quoted
and endorsed by those who are dissatisfied with what they
conceive to be the antiquated metaphysic of the ancient Church.
But it would not be at all an adequate reflexion of its author's
mind, as that may be discerned in his later writings.

Mr. W. H. Moberly's chapter on " The Atonement " was
eirenic in character, seeking to hold the balance between what
may be called " objective " and " subjective " views. The
notion of vicarious penitence which Mr. Moberly's father had
expounded was presented in, essentially, its original form.
The other contributors were Mr. Neville Talbot, Mr. R. G.
Parsons, Mr. A. E. J. Rawlinson, and Mr. R. Brook. It is not
easy to find a phrase to sum up the general tenor of *Foundations*,

" Critical orthodoxy " may come near it. The writers were certainly at one in their belief that the truth of Christianity, as the religion of the Incarnation, to use the words of the *Lux Mundi* sub-title, remained unaffected by New Testament criticism and by a not always approving estimate of the forms in which orthodox belief had been stated.

The book did not escape sharp criticism. A satirical poem by Mr. R. A. Knox, *Absolute and a Bit of Hell*, became famous, and he followed it up with a detailed criticism in *Some Loose Stones*. But no storm followed comparable with that which burst after the publication of *Essays and Reviews* and of Gore's essay in *Lux Mundi*, though Mr. Streeter's appointment by Dr. Percival, the Bishop, to a Canonry of Hereford did not pass without protest. It is not without significance, in relation to the theological and ecclesiastical history of the Church of England in the last twenty-five years, that of these seven Oxford men five have become Bishops: Dr. Temple, Bishop of Manchester and Archbishop of York and Canterbury, Dr. Parsons, Bishop of Southwark and Hereford, Dr. Talbot, Bishop of Pretoria, Dr. Rawlinson, Bishop of Derby, and Dr. Brook, Bishop of St. Edmundsbury and Ipswich.

Foundations was in no sense an Anglo-Catholic pronouncement, though one at least of the contributors, A. E. J. Rawlinson, might not improperly be described, as his chapter on " The Ministry and the Sacraments " suggested, as a Liberal Anglo-Catholic. But it may be regarded as pointing the way to a greater readiness on the part of some, though not all, Anglo-Catholics to adopt a far less conservative attitude towards New Testament criticism than had been customary. How far an Anglo-Catholic scholar can go in combining a defence of sacramental and devotional practices generally associated with the Church of Rome with a critical attitude towards the New Testament, that would once have been regarded as characteristic only of Liberal or Broad Church scholars, is apparent in the writings of Canon W. L. Knox, brother of R. A. Knox, and for many years a member of the Oratory of the Good Shepherd, Cambridge.

The movement of these younger men at Oxford was away from the more set and rigid forms of the Tractarian tradition. That tradition was represented on the philosophical side by Scott Holland, who became Regius Professor at Oxford in 1911;

on the Biblical side by Dr. Walter Lock, Warden of Keble; and in the regions of Church History and Patristic Theology by Dr. B. J. Kidd, who was to succeed Lock at Keble, by Cuthbert Turner, later Dean Ireland's Professor, and by the very learned Principal of Pusey House, Dr. Darwell Stone. Nor were there lacking younger men to carry the tradition on, particularly on its theological and ecclesiastical side, notably N. P. Williams, who took part a few years later (1916) in a notable controversy with the veteran Dr. Sanday, which was given to the public in a book with the title *Form and Content in the Christian Tradition.* Dr. Williams later occupied Dr. Sanday's old chair as Lady Margaret Professor of Divinity.

Evangelical theology, in the accepted sense of the phrase, was taught in Oxford by Dr. Griffith Thomas, Principal of Wycliffe Hall. Without definitely committing himself to a doctrine of complete Biblical inerrancy, Dr. Thomas undoubtedly inclined towards it. He was, it is not unfair to say, unsympathetic towards any departure from the doctrines of the sixteenth century Reformers, and any interpretation of Anglican formularies which did not emphasize a close connexion between Anglican theology and that which owed so much to Calvin. In his opposition, alike to the teaching about the Bible given by Higher Critics of the school of Driver, not to mention those who went much further than he, and to the doctrines of the Tractarians and their successors concerning the Church and the sacraments, Dr. Thomas was representative of a great body of Evangelical opinion. But, in relation to the Bible, there were signs of a changed attitude among a number of the younger men of this school of thought.

That which is now known as the Anglican Evangelical Group Movement had its beginnings in the years before the war. Such men as Principal Tait of Ridley Hall, Cambridge, and Principal Warman of St. Aidan's College, Birkenhead (later Bishop of Truro, Chelmsford, and Manchester), gave it their support. They and others would have entirely repudiated any idea that they were seeking to break away from the historic principles of the Reformation or the characteristic emphases of Evangelical theology. But they were not prepared to identify Evangelicalism with what we now call Fundamentalism; they did not regard the unique place and authority of the Bible as

necessarily involving a denial of the conclusions which such
scholars as Driver, H. E. Ryle, G. A. Smith, and A. S. Peake
had reached in their researches into questions of date and authorship, and in their attempts to distinguish and to evaluate the
materials used by the Biblical writers. In their sacramental
views they made no approach to the doctrines of the High
Church party, but they were anxious to make it clear that
Evangelicalism was not without its own strong and positive
sacramental theology. It would, of course, be quite unfair to
suggest that Evangelicalism had, in the previous century, been
indifferent to the sacraments; but the stress had not fallen upon
them. The Liberal Evangelicals, as they are now called, have
become an increasingly influential group within the Church of
England, and a number of the Bishops would be more naturally
described by that title than by any other. Something more
will need to be said about them, as we come to the present
situation.

In the English Free Churches the " New Theology " controversy had by this time died down. Mr. Campbell and his supporters had never had the notable theologians of the Free
Churches on their side. More and more during these years
did P. T. Forsyth stand out as teacher and writer on dogmatics.
He was not the greatest of technical scholars, and he was not
comparable in the sphere of religious philosophy with Dr.
A. M. Fairbairn, the Principal of Mansfield College, Oxford.
But there was a deep religious passion as well as theological
competence of the highest order in the succession of books
in which he expounded the atoning work of Christ. In Scotland
substantially the same doctrine of objective redemption was
being powerfully set forth by Dr. James Denney, though his
approach was more particularly Biblical and his theology more
akin to that which among the Protestant divines of the sixteenth and seventeenth centuries took the form of penal substitution. At the same time, and notably with Forsyth, there
was no return to former conceptions of Biblical infallibility.
It is, further, to be noted that while Forsyth belonged quite
definitely to the Reformation line of theologians and could be
sharply critical of Catholicism, both Roman and Anglican, he
had both an understanding of, and a respect for, the Catholic
tradition beyond what was common among Free Church theolo-

gians. With an undogmatic Christianity he had no sympathy at all, and he saw in the manifestations of its spirit a far more deadly danger than existed in the Catholic system. His neighbour in Hampstead, Dr. R. F. Horton, was at this time at the height of his powers as a preacher and as an exponent of an Evangelical interpretation of Christianity that could welcome a Liberalism which was firm in its confession of Christ as the divine Lord and Saviour. He had no sympathy with the typical Catholic outlook and, it might be maintained, little understanding of it.

CHAPTER III

FROM 1914 TO THE PRESENT DAY

TO none did the first world-war come as a greater shock than to those who had appreciated the achievements of Germany in the fields of theological research. The names of such men as Harnack, Deissmann, Loofs, Jülicher, Wernle, Herrmann, and of others scarcely less eminent, had become as well known in England and Scotland as those of native scholars, and their influence had been a notable fact. Sanday's writings are the best proof of this, though, with all his attention to the tendencies of German thought, he never lacked the will and power to point out failings characteristic of even the most learned and least erratic of German scholars. It would be quite a mistake to imagine that the war led to a general turning away from German theology. Scholarship, even in the most difficult times, remains international, although circumstances may prevent any direct association between scholars. But, undoubtedly, the prestige that had belonged to the great Germans, almost in virtue of their being Germans, came to an end. In quarters hostile to the Liberal Protestantism of Harnack and his fellows, which was still the dominant tradition in the German Universities and was far better known in England than the older-fashioned and more conservative Lutheranism of Zahn and Kähler, the failure of a liberalized Christianity, which had broken with the dogmatic standards of Catholic Christianity, was sometimes heavily underlined. It would be obvious to-day that an equitable judgment on such a matter could not be passed in a time of war. But it would be true to say that after the outbreak of war the high-water mark of German influence upon British theological scholarship and opinion declined, and has never regained its former level. German work in this sphere has such manifest excellences that it will always receive great consideration and leave its impress on much that is written by English and Scottish students of theology; but it is very unlikely, and is certainly not to be

47

desired, that an era of such concentrated attention to the pronouncements and theories of German scholars will return.

The war years were naturally not very fruitful in orderly,
constructive work. Many younger men who would have been
working at some particular field and testing their own capabilities
in this or that branch of learning were putting their religion
and its theology to the fiery test of battle: and with so much
of the world in a turmoil the tasks of the Church might seem
to be far removed from those which the theological scholarship
of the Universities would pursue. Nevertheless, there were
events of some importance; certain tendencies in thought
began to reveal themselves, while on the personal side nothing
was more remarkable than the increasing influence of the
teaching of one who was a layman, a Roman Catholic, and half
a German, Baron Friedrich von Hügel.

The discussion on miracles, and the question of the relation
of the ordained minister to the Creeds of the Church, continued
within the Church of England. The old Liberal or Broad Church
party had made of itself more of an organization through the
Churchmen's Union (later called the Modern Churchmen's
Union), while the monthly journal *The Modern Churchman*,
though not an official organ of the Union, was representative
of the general direction of the mind of this group. It had as its
editor Dr. H. D. A. Major, who had become Principal of Ripon
Hall, the theological College founded by the eloquent Broad
Church Bishop of Ripon, Dr. Boyd Carpenter. The College,
while keeping its name, was removed to Oxford in 1919. The
name "Modernist" was beginning to play a part as a description
of those whom the Churchmen's Union brought together;
this was hardly an improvement in terminology, since the movement, to which the title had first been given, was one within
the Roman Catholic Church, and the Anglican Modernists as
a whole were decidedly of the Liberal Protestant type. The
leaders, such men as Hastings Rashdall, who became Dean of
Carlisle in 1917, Professor Percy Gardner of Oxford, Canon
Glazebrook of Ely, and Dr. Major himself had very little sympathy
with the positions of Loisy, Tyrrell, and the Italian Modernists.
But to this extent a measure of agreement may be found, in the
claim made by Roman Catholic Modernists and Anglican Liberals
that the truth of Christianity was not bound up with any particular

conclusions which might be reached as a result of literary and historical study as to the miracles recorded in the Gospels; and both groups were at one in their belief that articles of the Creed which affirmed miracle might rightly be interpreted in a " symbolical " sense. In particular, they would not allow that a minister of the Church was precluded from such an interpretation. On the Anglican side this contention was further defended by the argument that the Creeds could not properly be held to possess any authority greater than that of the Scriptures. If, therefore, criticism of the Biblical narratives in which miracle appeared was legitimate, the same liberty must be exercisable in respect of the Creeds, which had no binding force beyond that which was theirs through their dependence upon Scripture.

The case of Dr. Hensley Henson, to which reference has been made above, has its place in the ecclesiastical history of the time, and is fully dealt with in the " Lives " of Randall Davidson and Charles Gore. It is unnecessary to enter here upon the personal aspects of the affair and the problems of discipline which might have involved a critical situation in respect of the relations between Church and State. From the strictly theological standpoint the case has a rather curious interest. It was held by a number of leading Churchmen, and particularly by Dr. Gore, that Dr. Henson had made a sharp separation of the miraculous element in the Gospels, in connexion with the birth and resurrection of Christ, from the doctrines of His incarnation and survival of death. Gore went so far as to express the view that Dr. Henson regarded the " physical miracles affirmed in the Creeds " as " incredible." Now, unquestionably Dr. Henson had argued for freedom for others. But even in his most outspoken remarks there was no definite statement of his own disbelief, a fact which the Archbishop, who handled the whole matter with a sympathy, insight, and tact of which few would have been capable, realized from the first. But the difficulty of the situation was greatly increased by an embarrassing letter of Dr. Sanday's to *The Times*, in which he identified Dr. Henson's attitude closely with his own. In this letter, without categorically denying the miraculous element, he spoke in such a way of " realistic expressions adapted to the thought of the time, of ineffable truths which the thought of the time could not express in any other way," that it was natural to conclude that he not

only desired freedom for those who could no longer accept
these " realistic expressions," but did himself think of them as
no longer valid. As I have said, it was never possible to be quite
sure of Sanday's actual belief; but of the effect of the letter
there could be no doubt. Dr. Henson was compromised altogether beyond what was right.

It was impossible that the matter should be left in that position.
Had that occurred, it would have appeared to many Churchmen
that consecration to a Bishopric in the Church of England was
compatible with definite disbelief in the miraculous events that
found a place in the Creeds. The situation was changed by the
memorandum prepared by the Archbishop as the result of a
conversation with Dr. Henson. In this statement Dr. Henson
affirmed that he worshipped Jesus Christ as " in the fullest
sense Divine," and believed that in His birth " there was
special action of the Holy Ghost "—which, it is right to remember, was the belief also of Dr. Sanday. But the closing sentences,
taken as a whole, are such as Sanday could not have made his
own. They run as follows: " But when in the Creed I affirm,
as I readily do, the traditional belief of the Church in the birth
of Jesus Christ without a human father, I am bound to add that
the belief in the Incarnation may be consistent now, as it was
consistent in Apostolic days, with other notions or explanations
of the mode of what happened therein. I have never seen any
satisfying alternative to the dogma of the Virgin Birth." The
question of the nature of assent to the Creeds was not definitely
answered; but there was no abandonment of the resolution set
out by the Bishops of the Province of Canterbury in 1914, when
the controversy about miracle and subscription was at its height.
In it, while they emphasized the need for considerate treatment
of the conclusions provisionally reached by reverent students,
they gave their " deliberate judgment that the denial of any
of the historical facts stated in the Creeds goes beyond the
limits of legitimate interpretation, and gravely imperils that
sincerity of profession which is plainly incumbent on the
ministers of the Word and sacraments."

How far this resolution has weighed with the Modernist
section of Anglican opinion is not easy to gauge. In one of the
best discussions of the doctrinal and disciplinary problem that
came from the Modernist side, the late Mr. Cyril Emmet's

Conscience, Creeds and Criticism (1918), stress is laid on the fact that the pronouncement was intended to be as " cautious and conciliatory as possible," and Mr. Emmet himself noted that while " denial " was condemned, " questioning " was not. It is probable that, from then till now, most of those who represent Modernist views, and desire that as much liberty as possible should be granted for the holding of those views within the Church of England, would accept the distinction just mentioned. At the same time it would be very difficult to show or to believe that the Modernist movement has been favourable to the affirmation of the miraculous events recorded in the Creeds.

In 1918 *The Faith of a Modern Churchman* appeared as the first volume in the " Modern Churchman's Library." It was issued under the auspices of the Churchmen's Union and its writer was Dr. Glazebrook. The argument was far more in line with a denial of the miracles than with any other attitude. The book received much attention. Dr. Chase, the Bishop of Ely, a learned New Testament scholar, replied to it at length, and the controversy between him and Dr. Glazebrook developed to considerable length. The question in debate was not simply as to " miracle " as generally understood. The deeper issue of the doctrine of the Incarnation was becoming clear. To opponents of the Modernist movement it has not been clear that the Modernists and themselves have really meant the same thing by that doctrine. The Modernist Christology has been suspected of a substantial, and not simply a formal, difference from that of St. Paul and St. John and the Nicene Creed, as, in effect, a doctrine of divine immanence at its highest point, but not one to which it would be proper to apply the words of the fourth Gospel that the Word was made flesh. Modernists, on the other hand, have contended that they have sacrificed nothing of permanent value in their attempt to state the truth of the Person of Christ with the help of ideas and the use of a terminology more familiar to this generation than is the philosophy and the language employed in the Creeds. Of this more will need to be said later on.

One of the inevitable consequences of the war of 1914-18 was to raise in an acute form the question of the relation of God to the suffering of the world. This was, of course, in no way a new problem. J. R. Illingworth had written on the subject in the chapter he contributed to *Lux Mundi*. But the scale and concentration of suffering for which the war was responsible made a profound impression on many deeply religious minds: and to many of them the notion that God did not share in that suffering seemed to be intolerable. It was natural and suitable that the denial of that notion in the strongest and even fiercest way should come not from an approved scholar or theologian but from a chaplain who knew at first hand the terrors and cruelties and devastations of war. G. A. Studdert-Kennedy had been given leave of absence from his parish in Worcester to take up the work of a chaplain at the front. Various features of his personality combined to make him an outstanding figure among Army chaplains. In 1918 his first book, *The Hardest Part*, was published. The title was meant to express in arresting manner the belief that in the experience of suffering it was God, not man, who had most to endure. The book was written under the stress of personal immersion in the war, and its emotional aspect is largely due to that fact. But it would be quite a mistake to suppose that Studdert-Kennedy was a man of heart at the expense of head. He was a fine and very honest thinker, though not of the academical type, and what he wrote in *The Hardest Part* remained a deep conviction from which he never went back.

The question with which he dealt had already begun to be discussed by theologians. C. E. Rolt had affirmed the truth of the suffering God in his book, *The World's Redemption* (1913), and B. H. Streeter in an article in the *Hibbert Journal* in 1914. As to what was involved in the idea there was much variation of outlook, and expositors of it could state it in what was to those who did not accept it at all different degrees of unacceptability. It may be noted that many years before the war Dr. Fairbairn had declared, in a phrase whose very extravagance revealed the strength of his feeling, that there was no falser idea in theology than that of the impassibility of God. The interest in the subject and the modern reaction, which in some cases seemed almost to amount to an unquestioning belief in divine passibility, are reflected in the historical survey which the present writer made in his book *The Impassibility of God*, which grew out of a survey of the subject undertaken for the Doctrinal Commission appointed by the Archbishops.

For some time before the war there had been an increasing attention to the subject of religious experience. The writings of Dr. Inge and of Evelyn Underhill had familiarized many with the ideas that may broadly be described as mystical, though it would be a mistake to suppose that they, or others who dealt with this subject, identified religious experience with the special characteristics of mysticism. But the greatest work on the subject came from the Roman Catholic layman, von Hügel, who was already known as the friend of some of the most prominent Modernist teachers, and was, at least to some extent, sympathetic with their efforts. *The Mystical Element of Religion* was first published in 1908, and its importance was immediately recognized. Especially has its analysis of the three strands in religion, the institutional, the experimental, and the intellectual, had wide influence. Worthy of special notice in connexion with von Hügel's theology and its relation to the work of other writers who, like him, were working at the field of religious experience, is the fact of his extremely firm grasp of the doctrine of divine transcendence. On the whole, the stress upon experience accords with an emphasis upon divine immanence, since the characteristics of that experience can readily be regarded as resulting from the presence of the divine " spark," the *Funkelein*, as Meister Eckhart called it, within the soul. And though such a conception does by no means necessarily lead on to a pantheistic confusion of God with man (of Eckhart Dr. Inge says in his Bampton Lectures that " the question has been much debated whether Eckhart really falls into pantheism or not "), it is easy to see how its natural association is with a strongly immanental notion of God. The tendency to substitute an insistence upon experience for an insistence upon authority, which Archbishop Frederick Temple towards the end of his life noted as a probable development, is in line with this attention to the doctrine of immanence. Moreover, the attempt to interpret Christian theology from the evolutionary standpoint pointed in the same direction. These tendencies found particular illustration in the controversy over the " New Theology." One of Dr. Gore's criticisms of Mr. Campbell's position was that his teaching, as given in such sayings as that " The real God is the God expressed in the universe and in yourself," and that there is no " dividing line between our being and God's," left little room for " the thought of God as self-complete and beyond and above the universe."

As against any one-sided stress upon immanence von Hügel stood absolutely firm. It was this as much as anything, on the strictly doctrinal side, which made a barrier between him and some, at least, of the most influential Modernist leaders. Anyone who wishes to appreciate von Hügel's mind on this subject should read the chapter on " The Idea of God " in the *Essays and Addresses on the Philosophy of Religion* (Second Series), delivered originally in August 1918 at a memorable meeting of the Anglican Fellowship. There, von Hügel's disagreement with Pringle-Pattison's theology as expounded in the Gifford Lectures of 1912-13, entitled *The Idea of God in the Light of Recent Philosophy*, turns upon the inadequacy of the Professor's notion of divine transcendence. With much that Pringle-Pattison said he had deep sympathy, but he could not come to terms with whatever involved the conclusion that in some way God's existence depended upon the existence of the world. In opposition to teaching of a Hegelian character which would conceive of the Absolute as being, not God in independence of the world, but God *and* the world, or God *and* finite spirits, von Hügel affirmed that " God does not require finite beings nor the universe to attain to self-consciousness or self-articulation; whereas all finite spirits and the universe strictly require God for their various degrees of reality and consciousness."

It is interesting to note that Mr. C. C. J. Webb in his *God and Personality*, which is the first course of his Gifford Lectures of 1918 and 1919, the period to which von Hügel's address belongs, criticizes " the statement in which recent philosophers of very various schools in this country have concurred that ' God is not the Absolute,' " since its result, " if taken seriously," would be to " make nonsense of religion." I am not trying to identify the theology of these two eminent philosophers, but each in his own way taught a doctrine of divine transcendence, with which the affirmation of divine personality is closely related, and each was sensitive to the requirements of religious experience. With " the demand of the religious consciousness for an immanent God " Mr. Webb was wholly in sympathy, and a difference of emphasis and, to some extent, of outlook between him and von Hügel must be admitted at this point; but the balance of his statements, with his vindication of the notion of personality as applied to God, leaves a very different impression from that which the sentences quoted above and others like them produced upon Dr. Gore when he was reading *The New Theology* some ten years earlier. By 1918 Mr. Campbell's own position had changed. He had abandoned those elements in his teaching which were clearly incompatible with the historic orthodoxy of the Christian Church, and in 1916 he was ordained deacon and priest in the Church of England.

The importance of von Hügel's combination of a profound interest in religious experience and mysticism with an unswerving adherence to the doctrine of God as that had been presented in the traditional theology of the Christian Church has been great. The best illustration of this fact would be found in the later writings of Miss Evelyn Underhill, who has probably done more than any other writer to interpret the nature of religious experience to numbers of people. Miss Underhill is immensely in the debt of von Hügel. That is not, of course, to make the absurd suggestion that she is an unoriginal retailer of his views. But it may be doubted whether the proportion of her teaching, especially in its more technically theological aspects, would not have been seriously affected had she not come so much under the influence of von Hügel. It is significant that in her book *Worship* (1936), in the Library of Constructive Theology, one of the last things she wrote, there are far more references in the Index of Persons to von Hügel than to any other theologian.

The extent of von Hügel's contribution to the theology of his age could be determined only by a survey of a mass of literature. And while there may have been a tendency, particularly in some Anglican circles, to look upon him as almost beyond criticism, his writings have probably done more than those of any other teacher to revive the sense of the grandeur of the Christian doctrine of God and of the depth and manifoldness of the Christian religion. No one has estimated his influence more highly than Dr. Inge.

Of Dr. Inge himself it may be said that while his sayings and writings were making him very well known in wide circles, and gaining for his religious, political, and sociological views an attention which no other English theologian received to at all the like extent, his importance in the field of the philosophy of religion was finally fixed by his Gifford Lectures on *The Philosophy of Plotinus*, delivered in the University of St. Andrews in 1917 and 1918. In the retrospect of his life, published in 1934, the year when he ceased to be Dean of St. Paul's, under the title, *Vale*, Dr. Inge speaks of " the honey of Plotinus " which was " carried off to the Christian hive " by Augustine and pseudo-Dionysius, to such a degree that Plotinus " almost belongs to the evolution of Christian philosophy." This is a very significant, and would be regarded by some as a very controversial, remark. Dr. Inge has always stood in sharp opposition to Harnack and those who have contended that the Greek influence upon Christian doctrine resulted in an obscuring of the true Gospel and its " intellectualizing " through the incoming of alien forms of thought. On this question there would be little difference between Dr. Inge and the *Lux Mundi* school, widely as in more definitely ecclesiastical matters he would be at variance with them.

But it is to be noted that in the last twenty-five years the value of the Greek contribution to Christian thought has been directly or indirectly attacked from a standpoint other than that which Harnack and the Ritschlians, and Liberal English theologians like Hatch, represented. The exposition of Christianity which we associate with Karl Barth and his school on the Continent, and with the late Sir Edwyn Hoskyns in England, is characterized by a deep suspicion of the tendency to present Christianity as a philosophy of religion. Wherever the metaphysical interest in religion, which owes more to Greece than to any other country, is in the ascendant, it is natural to expound Christianity as the supremely true philosophy, as a rational scheme which is open to investigation by the human reason. In their opposition to this point of view the Barthians revive the hostility which Luther felt towards the humanism of Erasmus. It would be going too far to say that Hoskyns was at one with them in this hostility; but undoubtedly the effect of his work was to concentrate attention on those elements in Christianity which the philosopher finds refractory if not irrational, and to underline those elements as of the very substance of the Gospel. On the other hand, Barth and Hoskyns have shown no hesitation in accepting the formulations of orthodoxy worked out by the patristic theologians and incorporated in the Nicene Creed. They have no sympathy with Hatch's notion of the substitution of a philosophy for the original Gospel. Barth protests most strongly against the idea that the Nicene theology can be dispensed with as though it represented the intrusion of philosophy on the soil of the Gospel. " Care should be taken," he writes in his book *Credo*, wherein he expounds the various clauses of the Apostles' Creed, " to avoid regarding this presupposition of the Biblical witness [i.e., that God in the Person of His Son bridges the abyss between Himself and man] (which after all Dogma does no more than make explicit) as a metaphysic superfluous and alien to Christian faith, and therefore getting rid of or emasculating it."

The question of the right relation between Biblical theology and philosophy is one of the most vital with which a theologian may concern himself, and it is no part of the present work to enter upon any discussion thereof. But the subject cannot be dismissed without a special reference to the work of Dr. Inge. It has been his constant purpose to set forth and to appreciate the rational character of Christian theology. And in his own person he shows the great difficulties which attend on any attempt to define with exactness the meaning of the words " modernism " and " modernist." One who can say that he has " a great admiration for the old Catholic philosophy of religion, of which St. Thomas Aquinas is the most learned exponent," is at that point, which is not situated on the circumference of religious belief, as far removed from some who would claim the name of " modernist " as he is from Karl Barth.

There is a difference of great importance between the theology, as well as the theological politics, of the present age and that of the end of the nineteenth century and the earlier years of the twentieth. It is, of course, true that various reservations need to be made, and that tendencies in theology are no less apt to be confused by cross-currents than those which are observable in connexion with other subjects; but it remains possible to note and describe certain tendencies as dominant and as exercising the strongest influence in the whole theological field. I will try to set down these tendencies briefly and perhaps crudely before any attempt is made to relate them to particular movements and writings.

First, then, these years have been marked by an increasing sense of the need for theological synthesis. This is the intellectual counterpart of the desire for a unity in which the outward form shall correspond to the inner spirit, and Christians shall effectively realize in what they do within the Church that they are one body in Christ. And just as the underlining of ecclesiastical differences in any controversial manner has almost entirely ceased, so has the controversial note largely disappeared from theology. That is not to say that all theological questions are in process of being settled, and that on all subjects where contradictions and hesitations have been continually in evidence general agreement is now in sight. But characteristic of the theology of this age is the recognition that the statement of opposite positions, and the controversial handling of them, is a stage beyond which it is necessary to pass. A preference for the formula " Both . . . And " rather than for that other formula " Either . . . Or " goes along with a tacit acknowledgment of the large amount of truth expressed in the saying that men are mostly right in what they affirm and wrong in what they deny. Clearly, such formulas as these are valid only up to a point. The Barthians show plainly enough, if concrete evidence is needed, that the element of contrast and opposition cannot be rooted out of theology. The capacity for saying " Yes " involves also the capacity for saying " No "; and that capacity is not one that merely lies in reserve as an ultimate safeguard of truth, which, nevertheless, may never be brought into action. If theology were to be regarded as positive only in its affirmations and not also in its denials, it would be difficult to justify the contrast inherent in Christian theology between itself and all other theologies. So, within Christian theology we must not shut our eyes to real oppositions which cannot be smoothed out, as though they represented no more than misunderstandings by each of the opposing theologians or groups of what the other is intending to affirm, or survivals from a time when statements and counter-statements stood for genuine and irreconcilable differences. But if we are trying to describe the theological temper of to-day, it is as eirenic, not controversial, that we shall appreciate its quality; and the impulse at work is one that finds no satisfaction in the marshalling of anti-thesis over against thesis, but seeks to discover a synthesis in which justice is done to the two apparently contrary positions.

Dr. O. C. Quick's book, *Catholic and Protestant Elements in Christianity*, published in 1924, was typical, not of what many people were writing but of the standpoint after which many people were feeling, even if they had not arrived at it. Two sentences taken from the opening pages of the book would meet with far wider assent to-day than at any time between the age of the Reformation and the the outbreak of the European War in 1914. Speaking of the gains accruing from controversy, when controversy is directed to its proper ends of an understanding of differing ideas and of an appreciation of the values which give to the ideas " life and power," he declares that " to grasp the central idea within a system of thought to which one is opposed, is to cease to desire to destroy that system altogether, and to seek rather to preserve and to vindicate the essential value wherein its real strength lies." In these words controversy as a weapon of mere and sheer destruction is condemned and abandoned, while the use of a method which is certainly in part controversial is justified in the explanation that " it is the aim of these lectures to elicit and to define some of the different values for which Catholicism and Protestantism have stood, to set them first in opposition and antithesis to one another, and then to suggest that reconciliation is both a need and a possibility."

Secondly, I would lay stress on the increasing attention given to, and the greater emphasis laid upon, Biblical theology. What I have already written with regard to Dr. Inge and Sir Edwyn Hoskyns bears upon this point. It is obvious to all who are acquainted with the work of both that Hoskyns was a Biblical theologian in a sense that could not be affirmed of Dr. Inge: and the importance of Hoskyns as teacher and writer has been very great in this connexion. But it is to no one scholar or theologian that this stress upon Biblical theology is due. It is to some extent the reverse side of the " stumbling-block," which undoubtedly the Biblical ideas present to many, whose whole world of thought is controlled by conceptions which they gain from the natural sciences. But the Church can no more afford to hide this stumbling-block away than in the first age it could remove from the eyes of Jews and Greeks that other " scandal " of the Cross. No compromise is possible here: after all, Christian theology *is* Biblical theology, and the Christian Church cannot but stand to it, and the more definitely and unflinchingly because of the obstacles which it offers to a generation too often ignorant of the Bible. That is not to say that the world of Biblical ideas should be presented as though it were one between which and the world of current and scientific conceptions nothing but hostility could exist. But the first thing to be done about it is to proclaim it. Such a proclamation was made by Christian preachers in Germany in the face of the attempt to expound religion in terms of race. Both Cardinal Faulhaber and Pastor Niemöller opposed to that attempt the religious outlook of the Bible. In doing so they have been representative of that *communis sensus* which unites Christians in an affirmation of the truth of the Biblical theology, however much they may be divided in various matters affecting the authority and use of the Bible.

Thirdly, the emphasis upon Biblical theology is, more particularly, an emphasis upon that which supplies the central theme of such theology, namely the Gospel of God's redemptive action as the divine answer to man's sin. Witness has been borne to this by one who has made no small contribution to it. In his primary charge (1937) to the clergy of the diocese of Derby Dr. Rawlinson speaks of himself as " profoundly encouraged by the manifest signs which are all about us, in the world of modern theology, of a fresh, constructive and positive grasp of the essential Gospel of Christianity, and of a renewed apprehension and understanding of the ancient doctrines of Sin, and of Atonement, and of Redemption." The influence of Barth must be ungrudgingly acknowledged in this connexion; whatever be thought of his theology in some of its characteristic moments, without doubt he has done much to turn the minds of Christian thinkers back to a deeper realization of the " ancient doctrines " on which the Bishop of Derby lays stress. But, so far as England is concerned, the movement towards a more insistent theological emphasis upon the Gospel, as a Gospel of redemption rather than of the union of the divine and the human through incarnation, was in progress before the name of Barth had begun to have significance for English scholars.

Fourthly, with this recovery, if so strong a word may be allowed, of due attention to the primacy which in the Bible belongs to the theology of grace, there has been associated a much less anxious attitude towards critical problems than obtained even a comparatively short time ago. That I should regard as applying not only to questions of date and authorship, but to those which arise around the historical content of the Biblical writings. Obviously this is a field in which wide differences are discernible; but if one tries to form a general impression of the existing situation, it would, I think, be near the truth to say that, with the exception of those who have committed themselves to that view of the Scriptures known as " Fundamentalist," theologians would not regard the affirmation of the authority of the Bible as involving one, and only one, judgment upon the historical accuracy of the Biblical narratives. It is not the case that the majority of British theologians have come to reject the miraculous element in the Gospels, and to regard it as of merely symbolic value; but many, if not most, of them would be unwilling to think of the truth of the Gospel as bound up with that element. It is too early to say that this attitude is likely to be permanent. It may become clear that Gore, and those whose outlook was similar to his, were right in their view that full Christian faith in Christ cannot be separated from the affirmation of miracle. But I am concerned with a prevailing tendency, as that appears to have developed between the two world-wars; and as to that the facts would seem to be as I have tried to state them.

The last matter which comes within the field of this attempted survey of changes in the direction of theological thought concerns the doctrine of the Church and the sacraments. Herein of the first importance is the much greater stress upon the Church as itself an article of Christian faith among those whose interest in theology has seemed to stop short of the Church. It is easy both to misread and to exaggerate in relation to this question. There can be no suggestion of any indifference to the doctrine of the Church on the part of such men as Dale and Forsyth; and among Free Churchmen generally there was doubtless far more of a " Church sense " than an Anglican, with his external position, would realize. But it might not be unfair to suggest that attention was not in a marked degree given to the doctrine of the Church by the majority of Free Church divines. In this respect things have changed. That is due to a variety of causes. World-politics have forced the question of the Church into the foreground, particularly in Germany; and that has meant a persistent recall to Christians to view the problem of Church and State or Church and Nation in relation to the nature of the Church. Again, and with the world-situation still in view, the apprehension of the need for Christian unity has made it entirely necessary to take the doctrine of the Church with the utmost seriousness. For Christian unity, as it has been understood and longed for by Christians of very different backgrounds, organized in distinct societies, has meant Church unity. The great Conferences of Lausanne in 1927 and Edinburgh in 1937, which met to discuss questions of Faith and Order, and, further, the Oxford Conference on Life and Work in 1937, would never have met had it not been realized that a theology of the Church is indispensable, both for Christian thinking and for Christian practice.

It would hardly be going too far to say that the opening words of Sir Edwyn Hoskyns' article, " The Christ of the Synoptic Gospels," in *Essays Catholic and Critical* would meet now with a large measure of agreement from many theologians who are not Anglicans and differ from Anglo-Catholics on not a few doctrinal and practical issues. Hoskyns wrote, " For the Catholic Christian *Quid vobis videtur de Ecclesia, What think ye of the Church ?* is not merely as pertinent a question as *Quid vobis videtur de Christo, What think ye of Christ ?*: it is but the same question differently formulated." It is the approach to a common mind in respect of the identification which Hoskyns declared to exist which is of so great importance. Christians, whether they be scholars or not, are still a long way from agreement as to what is or should be the true doctrine of the Church. It is the sense of the necessity for a doctrine of the Church, or, if that be too definitely stated, of due attention to the clauses in the Creeds which express the Christian's belief in the Holy Catholic Church, that has been rediscovered.

And it is not just a case of the position in which the Church finds itself in the world to-day compelling Christians to think about Christian unity, and therefore about a theology of the Church. It is the increased insight into the theology of the Bible and especially of the New Testament which has set the Church in the forefront of dogmatic interest. It is no mere individual opinion that Dr. Garvie gave in his book, *The Christian Faith* (1936), when he spoke of the community constituted by the " common possession " of the Holy Spirit, which works as the body of Christ and is destined to become the temple of God, as " not to be regarded as a human device and invention, but as a divine Creation, continuing not only the first creation of man, but also the second creation in the Incarnation." The final words are, indeed, simply a different way of expressing that truth to which Anglican High Churchmen have witnessed in the phrase, " The Church is the extension of the Incarnation." Nor would there be only a few to echo Dr. Garvie's moving confession in the same chapter that " imperfect Christian as I am, I know that I have become a better Christian than I was since this ideal of the one Church has become the constant inspiration of my thoughts and life in sharing in œcumenical movements."

The Church is the Church that worships, even as it is the Church that witnesses and teaches and evangelizes. But worship belongs to the corporate life of the Church in a more obvious way than do its functions of preaching and instruction. It is natural that those who have made much of that corporate life should have laid great stress upon the worship of the Church, and devoted much time to the study of its character and method. And because of the special place occupied in relation to worship by the sacraments, and especially by the Eucharist, the meaning and value and relevance of the sacraments have received a fullness of consideration over and above that which belongs to them in virtue of their dogmatic significance. This attention has been given for the most part by those who represent the Catholic side of the Christian tradition. But there are signs of an increasing interest in sacramental theology and worship on the part of those who would lay stress on their Evangelical and Protestant background. It is natural at this point once more to remind any who may need it that a concern for sacramental doctrine was not restricted during the last century and in the years that followed it to Anglicans, and, more narrowly, to Anglo-Catholics. Dale taught what some regarded as a dangerously " high " doctrine of the Lord's Supper; Forsyth conceived of no error with regard to that sacrament as so deadly as that which made of it a mere memorial service; while even if the Scottish divines, Dr. Wotherspoon and the Rev. J. M. Kirkpatrick, are offering their own interpretation of the Eucharist, when in their book, *A Manual of Church Doctrine* (1919), they say that " the Sacrament is thus at once the highest act of worship and the chiefest means of grace,'' they are evidence of an attitude towards the Eucharist which may be paralleled in the late Dr. R. S. Simpson's Chalmers Lectures, *Ideas in Corporate Worship*, lectures delivered in 1922. Forsyth and Simpson would have refused to think of themselves as in any way free lances or unrepresentative of a Church tradition. But I think it is difficult to conceive of such a work as the volume of essays entitled *Christian Worship*, which was put out in 1936 by members of Mansfield College, as appearing so early as Simpson's Chalmers Lectures or as Forsyth's *Lectures on the Church and the Sacraments* (1917).

But there is another side to this deepened interest in the theology of the Church and the sacraments on the part of those whose *natural* concern would, in the opinion of many, be directed rather to other aspects of Christian doctrine. Whereas the first Tractarians and their successors (such a man as Liddon is an obvious instance) possessed and insisted on a precise and even rigid doctrine of the Church, with its ministry and sacraments, some, at least, of those who would claim, in general, to follow in the lines of the Tractarian tradition would find it necessary to make a number of reservations before they could affirm the Tractarian theology on this subject. It is probable that the younger Anglo-Catholic theologians would feel the need for more elasticity both on the historical and on the doctrinal side, for less confident affirmations both as to the results to be reached from a study of the Biblical material and of the primitive Christian writings, and as to the doctrinal conclusions to be drawn from research into these sources. These considerations apply especially to the whole question of the ministry. Those whom I have in mind would not deny the truth of the doctrine of apostolical succession, on which the first of *Tracts for the Times* laid such stress, nor doubt that the succession of ministers within the Church is duly maintained through the instrumentality of episcopal ordination. But they would not be ready, as the Tractarians were, and as theologians like Dr. Gore and Dr. Darwell Stone, who stood within the strict Tractarian tradition, were, to assert the doctrine of apostolical succession in one particular form, namely as a transmission of grace from consecrator to consecrated; nor would they affirm the episcopate to be essential to the *esse* of the Church in such a way that any

Christian society which lacked the episcopate would thereby fall outside the Body of Christ and the covenant of grace. They would not approach the question of the *status* of the Church of Scotland with its presbyterian ministry, or of the Church of Finland, where in 1885 the episcopal succession could not, owing to political reasons, be carried on by episcopal consecration, with the same presuppositions as were characteristic of their predecessors.

It is interesting to compare the language of Dr. Gore, in relation to this whole question, with that of one who belonged very definitely to the same school of thought, but was not prepared to follow out its principles to those negative deductions from which theologians of an earlier period did not shrink. Dr. E. J. Bicknell, in his well-known work, *A Theological Introduction to the Thirty-Nine Articles of the Church of England*, writes as follows: " How then does the Church of England regard Nonconformist ministrations ? Stress should be laid on the positive rather than on the negative side. We are bound to hold fast to our ministry to secure the validity of our own ministrations. But the true antithesis to ' valid ' in such cases is not ' invalid ' but rather ' precarious.' We are convinced that Nonconformist rites are irregular: they have not on them the stamp of approval of the whole Church. But we have no wish to dogmatize on their position in the sight of God, or to deny that He employs them as means of grace. God is not limited to His ordinances, but we are."

Now it is true that a Nonconformist would not find any very generous admission as to the nature of Nonconformist ministries in these words. He would, perhaps, see in them simply the conception of uncovenanted mercies that would be familiar to him in the pages of many Anglo-Catholic writers, and he might take it to be the normal Anglo-Catholic view of the matter. But if such an one turned to the final chapter of Dr. Gore's book, *The Church and the Ministry* (1st Edition, 1888, revised by C. H. Turner, 1919), he would, were he attentive to the precise wording and the atmosphere which surrounds it, feel that Gore's emphasis upon the negative results which follow upon his historical survey is expressed with a confidence that is not present in Bicknell's pages. For after affirming that " it is absolutely certain that for a large number of centuries

5

it had been understood beyond all question that only Bishops could ordain and that presbyters had not episcopal powers," he goes on to say, " it follows then—not that God's grace has not worked, and worked largely, through many an irregular ministry where it was exercised or used in good faith, but— that a ministry not episcopally received is invalid, that is to say, falls outside the conditions of covenanted security, and cannot justify its existence in terms of the covenant." The assurance with which Gore writes, an assurance that was part of the secret of his influence, is not equally obvious in Bicknell. And in general it may be said that Anglican theologians, who are, in their outlook and affinities, more or less definitely of the Anglo-Catholic school, are less ready than their predecessors to commit themselves to the conclusion that Christian societies which lack the episcopate are in no sense part of the Church, and have no real Christian ministries.

It is relevant at this point to refer to the often quoted words of the representatives of the Church of England on the Joint Conference with representatives of the Free Churches held at Lambeth Palace in 1923. They declared themselves prepared to say that " ministries which imply a sincere intention to preach Christ's Word and administer the sacraments as Christ has ordained, and to which authority so to do has been solemnly given by the Church concerned, are real ministries of Christ's Word and Sacraments in the Universal Church." This affirmation committed no others than the signatories, and it would be quite improper to suggest that it would win general acceptance from Anglo-Catholic theologians: but it certainly goes far beyond what one can conceive being admitted twenty years earlier by any Bishops and scholars, who stood on the High Church side of Anglicanism as distinctly as did Dr. Talbot, then Bishop of Winchester, Dr. Gibson, who had recently resigned the see of Gloucester, and Dr. Frere, recently Superior of the Community of the Resurrection. Their signatures imply that on the doctrine of the Church and the Ministry they could not bind themselves to the Tractarian scheme of thought in the rigidity both of its presuppositions and of its conclusions. They would not for a moment have allowed that episcopacy was an open question, or that the ministry of the Church did not need to stand within a succession going back to the Apostles, and, ultimately, to the Lord: but in their estimate of the facts of disunion and of the problem of reunion, neither the dogmatic principles from which they started nor the interpretation of the actual relevant historical events were just the same as those characteristic of the Anglo-Catholic movement in its earlier stages.

The eirenic theological tendency observable, though not to be exaggerated, with regard to doctrines of the Church and the Ministry, is present also in relation to the sacraments and especially the sacrament of the Lord's Supper. Here, also, a double movement has been, and continues, in process. For while an appreciation of sacramental thought and practice has become more manifest among Free Churchmen, Anglican theologians, whose sympathies and starting-point are Catholic rather than Evangelical or Modernist, have been endeavouring to pass beyond the old historic forms of thought and the divisions which resulted therefrom, and to state eucharistic doctrine in ways that would help towards intellectual agreement. This process can already be observed in the important, though difficult, book *Belief and Practice*, by Sir W. Spens, now Master of Corpus Christi College, Cambridge, published in 1915. The positive doctrine of the Real Presence put forward by Sir Will Spens was presented in terms of his conception of an object as a complex of opportunities of experience, while his exposition of the eucharistic sacrifice was bound up with his estimate of the Lord's solemn dedication of Himself at the Last Supper to be, on the Cross, the one true oblation for the sins of the whole world. The theme in its development is obviously one that needs expert theological consideration: here, its introduction is due to the fact that from the Anglo-Catholic side there came an attempt to disentangle eucharistic doctrine from the forms in which, on both sides, the controversy had been handled. Canon Oliver Quick's volume in the Library of Constructive Theology, *The Christian Sacraments*, is written from a standpoint philosophically different from Sir W. Spens'; but it also shows how a theologian of great penetration can approach and expound the doctrine of the eucharist in such a way as to make for a wider agreement.

It would be too much to say that the sharp divisions so noticeable in connexion with the eucharistic controversy at the end of the last century have disappeared. The Evangelicals, who would not wish to be described as "Liberal," would probably refuse to admit that a doctrine of the Real Presence, which involves the assertion of a true relation between the bread and the wine and the Lord's Body and Blood as effected through consecration and prior to reception, could rightly be held by loyal members of the Church of England; while some Anglo-Catholics would claim for that doctrine sole validity, as alone consonant with the primitive and historic doctrine of the whole Catholic Church. But the general tendency has been away from an emphasis upon differences and from an insistence upon exactness of dogmatic definition, whether positively or negatively. No one could truly contend that, whatever explanations be given on either side, the tradition represented by many of the theologians of the patristic age, along with those who, like Pusey and Gore, made a special appeal to their teaching, and the tradition represented in somewhat different forms by Calvin, Hooker, Waterland, and Westcott, had been brought to a common agreement. But the idea that the former tradition involved a materialistic conception of the Eucharist and the latter a doctrine of a " real absence " (to use the old catch-phrase) of Christ from the Eucharist would be far less widely affirmed than in the time of acute controversial discussion. And this carries with it a greater restraint on the question of the reservation of the consecrated Bread and Wine for the purpose of communion of the sick, and even as to extra-liturgical devotions in the presence of the reserved Sacrament.

That such devotions necessarily involve a false theology of the Eucharist would not be maintained by all of those who are not themselves favourable to them. Some theologians would urge that this is a matter which falls properly within the field of discipline, and that, as with other pious and devotional practices, its further consequences for Christian thinking and Christian piety must be taken into account. Such an attitude rests upon the belief that the appeal to eucharistic theology does not in itself provide the material for a satisfactory decision. The words of Dr. Rawlinson in his primary charge to the clergy of the diocese of Derby would meet with considerable assent. "I think it important," he declares, "to recognize that the desire and the impulse to treat the reserved Sacrament as a focus of devotional approach to our Lord is in no way bound up, of necessity, with any directly *doctrinal* issue.'' That is not to say that doctrinal questions are irrelevant: they obviously are not; it is the nature and extent of their relevance which needs and, in measure, secures attention. Differences at this point are entirely compatible with far deeper agreements on the strictly theological side.

So much by way of introduction to currents of thought in the world of theology between the two great wars. Doubtless these might be differently described and appreciated, and a writer's own point of view must give to what he thinks he sees a particular significance in which others will not follow him. But even if the features of the country are not adequately recounted, if too much is made of one contour, and others are ignored or but slightly scanned, I would suggest that these features are existent and that it is in the second and third decades of the century that they came into prominence. They are represented in schools of thought and in theological writings which reveal much variety among themselves in relation to the exposition of Christian doctrine. To a considerable extent they indicate the possession, or at least the forming, of a common mind among scholars who belong to different Christian communions. And that means that theology, of which many good Christians are highly suspicious if not definitely unappreciative, is making a contribution of great importance to the cause of Christian unity.

It has been characteristic of Anglican theology that, while it has been carried forward by the labours of men who have been recognizably of one or other particular school of thought, it has also owed an incalculable amount to thinkers whom it is almost impossible to think of in terms of one of the great lines of the post-Reformation Anglican tradition. If one's mind recalls such names as those of Gore and Moule and Rashdall, it is obvious enough that the theology of the first is representative of the High-Church, Anglo-Catholic, tradition, the second of the Protestant-Evangelical strain in Anglicanism, the third of the Liberal Broad-Church standpoint: nor are the historical derivations and affinities of each of the three difficult to show. Yet even in such comparatively clear-cut cases as these it is necessary not to press the distinctions too exactly. There are points at which each of the three may be seen, in accordance with the main tendencies of the tradition which he carries forward, to be in close agreement with the second as against the third. On the subject of the value to be attached to the miraculous in Christianity, Gore and Moule are near to one another, as neither of them is to Rashdall; in their general view of the nature and results of the inspiration of the Bible Gore and Rashdall adopt a position which Moule would not entertain; while in regard to their conception of the Church, the ministry, and the sacraments, Moule and Rashdall, in their affirmations and denials, stand over against Gore. Moreover, in their agreements and disagreements, allowance must be made for the differences in starting-points and in emphases. Of the relevance of these facts to theological developments in the era between the wars more will be said later on.

But there have been theologians of the first rank, in respect both of the quality of their own work and of the influence they have exerted, whom it is impossible to place within a particular tradition. F. D. Maurice is one; F. J. A. Hort is another. It is difficult to think of either of them as other than Anglican theologians; it is impossible to align either of them with one school of thought within the Church of England. And what is true of them is true also, if not quite in the same degree, of other thinkers. Such were Frederick Temple, whose greatness would have been more clearly revealed in the field of theology had opportunity allowed, and John Wordsworth, who adorned the see of Salisbury with his great learning, and such were Lightfoot and Westcott. And of those who were disciples of the Oxford Movement and never broke away from their fundamental agreement with the principles of the Movement, two, J. B. Mozley and R. W. Church, may fairly be ranked with those already named as instances of the power to combine loyalty to a tradition with an independence of judgment which removes from the affirmation of that loyalty any danger of its being exalted into a battle-cry.

Let us look more closely at the history of Anglican theology within these more recent years. The particular traditions remain: there has been nothing like a sharp break. Theologians may, for the most part, be classified as representative of one or other of them. Indeed, it might appear at first sight as though

both on the Anglo-Catholic side and on the Modernist side
the early years after the first war had brought a more intense
self-consciousness, and a determination to insist more stiffly
on those doctrinal positions for which each movement stood.
Following on the first London Congress of 1920 and various
provincial gatherings, the Anglo-Catholic Congress of 1923,
over which the late Bishop of Zanzibar, Dr. Frank Weston,
presided, caused a great stir. Dr. Weston himself, as theologian,
missionary statesman, and controversialist, was one of the most
remarkable figures of his time. The Kikuyu service of inter-
communion between Anglicans and non-Anglicans, the publication of *Foundations* and particularly Mr. Streeter's treatment
in that book of the Gospel narratives of the Resurrection, and
the appointment of Dr. Hensley Henson to the Bishopric of
Hereford, all led him to outspoken protest, and even to the
severing of all sacramental fellowship between himself and
Dr. Percival, the Bishop of Hereford, who had appointed Streeter
to one of the canonries in his cathedral. But he attended the
Lambeth Conference of 1920, and was one of those who gained
to a remarkable degree the ear of a Conference that was by
no means in general agreement with his distinctive doctrinal
and ecclesiastical positions: moreover, on the subject of Reunion
he was far from being an unconciliatory exponent of the Anglo-
Catholic attitude. Yet to many his chairmanship of the 1923
Congress must have suggested the likelihood of Anglo-Catholicism
developing on the lines of theological rigidity and of extreme
sacramentalism. The telegram which was sent from the Congress
to the Pope did not abate the misgivings of more moderate
Churchmen, and Dr. Weston's counsel to his audience that they
should fight for their tabernacles seemed to imply a readiness to
advise resistance to ecclesiastical authority, since reservation
in a tabernacle, as contrasted with an aumbry, was precisely
the form of reservation to which the Anglican Bishops as a
whole took the greatest exception. In fact, there was no such
suggestion in Dr. Weston's mind; he was quite unconcerned
with the conditions under which the Sacrament, as reserved,
should be kept, and spoke merely in terms of his own East
African practice.

There are aspects of the Anglo-Catholic movement after
the first world-war which it would be out of place to consider

here. But its theological tendencies have been of real importance. A study of the Congress programme of the year 1923, and of the papers provided at other meetings, shows that scholars and theologians whose work in Biblical and doctrinal fields was of the first importance were prepared to give the movement the support of their learning. In this there is nothing surprising for anyone who remembers the profound theological interest which moved the Tractarians and their successors. But the attention given to matters of Church order and, still more, of ceremonial did probably convey the impression that the High-Church or Anglo-Catholic party was not greatly concerned with the science of theology: and this impression, for all its exaggeration, was not simply erroneous. But in the years that followed the war the association with the new phase of the Anglo-Catholic movement of scholars who were studying fundamental problems of theology was one of the striking facts of the religious situation. Such men as E. G. Selwyn, then Editor of *Theology*, A. E. J. Rawlinson, then student of Christ Church, Oxford, Sir Edwyn Hoskyns of Corpus Christi College, Cambridge, K. E. Kirk of Trinity College, Oxford, E. J. Bicknell, and others of similar standing, gave their help in speech and writing. The fifty-two " Congress Books " had as their writers some of the best-known theologians, both older and younger, of the Church of England. Clearly a movement which could draw together such men as those already named and, of men of long-standing reputation, Dr. Gore, Canon T. A. Lacey, Dr. Darwell Stone, and Professor A. E. Taylor, could not be disregarded as though it had nothing to contribute in the region of theological principles.

And once again a volume of essays, covering with some fullness the ground of Christian doctrine, summed up a position at which a number of scholars, working from a standpoint common to them all, and representative of a great body of religious opinion, had arrived. *Essays Catholic and Critical* (1926), though it had not the special interest of *Lux Mundi* and made no such stir as the older book had done, was, nevertheless, significant for its generation in the same kind of way that *Lux Mundi* was for the end of the nineteenth century. In one respect it was indeed the more important of the two volumes, since it expressed the nature of an Anglican Liberal Catholicism more adequately, and

with closer relation to Biblical theology, than was at all possible
some forty years before. During those years the theological
field had been the scene of the conflicts which had developed
around the conceptions first of Liberal Protestantism and then
of Modernism in its Catholic form. Anglican scholarship
had grown far more receptive of influences that came to it
from without. Those influences, it would be true to say, the
men who wrote *Essays Catholic and Critical* knew at first hand,
whereas their predecessors had hardly reckoned with them at
all, and they wrote their book with the historical situation in
full view. The general standpoint of the book may be understood
best by a reading of the Preface which Dr. Selwyn, the Editor,
contributed to the third edition. In it he makes it clear that the
Liberal Catholicism expounded by the essayists is one consciously
and deliberately set forth in contradistinction from Roman
Catholicism, from Protestantism, especially of the modern
Liberal type, and from Modernism. The claim which Dr.
Selwyn was prepared to make for the Liberal Anglo-Catholicism
presented in the *Essays* was that " it represents the best expression at present available, in thought, worship, and life, of the
principles necessary to an ultimate synthesis."

With these words of Dr. Selwyn's in mind, it will be appropriate to try to describe the main features of the Anglo-
Catholicism which he and his colleagues, and others who are
substantially of the same school, have sought to formulate.
We may begin with the stress laid upon the preservation of the
essentially Catholic type of Christianity. This, so it is held, is
recognizable both on the doctrinal and on the devotional side.
Continuity is maintained with the Church of the first centuries,
the Church which was conscious of its own Catholicity and was
marked by a particular temper or *ethos* in respect of its faith
and life. This temper was of the nature of a continual experience,
and the appeal to experience of the Catholic type, as the deepest
and richest kind of Christian experience, is the characteristic
way in which the Anglo-Catholic statement of continuity has
been made. The argument from experience is one that allows
of considerable differences in the manner in which it is presented
and in the conclusions drawn from it: it would be a misjudgment
if it were supposed that all Anglo-Catholic theologians would
state and defend it in exactly the same way. Nevertheless, and

especially in relation to the question of authority, the emphasis upon experience has been very noticeable.

So we come to the conception of authority. Every type of Christianity has had to reckon with this problem. The various positions are familiar; there has been the appeal to the authority of the Church, or of the Bible, or of the inner light regarded as the witness of the Spirit within the heart of man. Such appeals have not been simply contraries, though in the controversies of the times they have given that impression. Moreover, the appeal to authority, whether of Bible or of Church, has been that of men who, differing as to the ultimate seat of authority, have been at one in their assumptions as to the way in which the response of the authority would be given. It was response through definite pronouncement on some particular subject, and the pronouncement was infallibly right. There was, in fact, an equation of authority with infallibility. This equation was stated most definitely in the decree of the Vatican Council of 1870 with regard to the infallibility of the Pope. The authority of the Pope was, under certain conditions, infallible authority: in other words, the Pope was, in those circumstances, infallible even as the Bible and the Church were infallible. It was not only the Bible, as many Protestant Christians had been disposed to think, nor the Bible *and* the Church, as had been the belief of the Tractarians, which possessed this power of speaking infallibly, and, thereby, of settling vexed questions by an entirely competent authority; the same power belonged to a particular individual when he made a pronouncement of this authoritative kind in the sphere of faith or morals.

It is this conception of authority which has been criticized and rejected by Anglo-Catholic theologians. Thus, Dr. Rawlinson in *Essays Catholic and Critical* writes:

" The rejection of the claim of the Roman Church to be possessed of authority in the form of what I have ventured to describe as an external and oracular guarantee of the intellectual truth of its doctrines carries with it, in the long run, the rejection of the purely oracular conception of religious authority altogether. Neither the oracular conception of the authority of the Bible, nor that of the authority of the œcumenical Councils and Creeds, is in a position to survive the rejection of the oracular conception of the authority of the Pope."

In a volume published in 1937, *The Gospel of God and the Authority of the Church*, the Rev. W. L. Knox and the Rev. A. R. Vidler,

of the Oratory of the Good Shepherd, Cambridge, adopt a
position identical in its character with that of Dr. Rawlinson's
essay. They notice, only to show how entirely they dissociate
themselves from, the conception of an authority which has the
power to make infallible pronouncements. " The infallible
utterance of an oracular Church, the infallible certainty of the
guidance of the group by the Holy Spirit, or even a quaint return
to the doctrine of the letter of the Scriptures—these are forms
of authority which seek to commend themselves at the present
day." This is, it may be said, the language of controversy,
and it does not cover a positive doctrine of authority. It is,
indeed, probable that these two writers go further than most
Anglo-Catholics would in their repudiation of the whole idea
of inerrancy in relation to authoritative pronouncements.
But they are representative of a way of looking at the question
quite different from that which would have been tolerable to
the Tractarians or natural to the authors of Lux Mundi.

As to the relation between Christian religious experience
and Christian doctrine, the Anglo-Catholic view, as stated or
implied in the teaching of those who have given special attention
to this question, is that the broad lines of the Catholic dogmatic
do most justice to the experience, and conversely that it is the
Catholic doctrinal system which mediates the richest kind of
religious experience. Moreover, the characteristic Catholic
stress upon the Church as the body of Christ, and upon the
sacraments as channels of grace, is held to be in line with the
New Testament outlook, though the thought-forms of the New
Testament cannot be used to-day in exactly the same way as was
possible in the first centuries. So at the end of his contribution
to Essays Catholic and Critical, " The Christ of the Synoptic
Gospels," Sir Edwyn Hoskyns wrote: " There seems no reason
to doubt that the characteristic features of Catholic piety have
their origin in our Lord's interpretation of His own Person
and of the significance of His disciples for the world."

It is natural to ask how these developments in Anglo-
Catholicism were being regarded by those who still remained to
witness in their own persons to the Catholicism of the Lux
Mundi school, especially by him whose theological interests were
unabated and his powers hardly impaired, Dr. Charles Gore.
That Gore felt himself to be out of touch with the younger men

of the tradition that meant so much to him would be to speak
more positively than the facts would justify: but, undoubtedly,
he felt a certain tension in more directions than one. On the
strictly doctrinal side he was unprepared to make any advance
towards a " symbolic " interpretation of articles of the Creed
which dealt with questions of historical fact. His position was
well known, and had remained unchanged through all the controversial exchanges of the previous twenty and more years.
It was a position that some of those who were in their general
outlook on religion definitely Anglo-Catholics found un-
acceptable. They were not satisfied with his clear-cut distinction
between clauses in the Creed, and were not ready to commit
themselves on historical questions in the way that was characteristic of Gore. Neither in the middle twenties nor now would
the majority of Anglo-Catholic theologians have repudiated
Gore's insistence upon the historical fact of our Lord's Virgin
Birth and of the resurrection of His Body from the tomb.
But a difference on the question of miracle, which does not
stop short at any point in the Biblical narratives, has come to
exist within Anglo-Catholicism: and this is undoubtedly a change.
It is not surprising that this has been noted by Roman Catholic
critics as, at least, the beginning of the permeation of Anglo-
Catholicism by Modernism, nor that with this judgment
there should be some agreement in modernist circles.

It is worth while to try to state the problem with some
preciseness, since the differences which exist have reference
both to the substance of Christian doctrine and to the grounds
on which that doctrine is to be believed, in other words to
the nature of the authority rightly ascribable to the Creeds.
As to the former question, the difference concerns the necessity
of the particular fact if the doctrine is to be credible. Now
that some particularity is necessary all Christians would agree
(or, if here, as almost always, one must say " not quite all,"
the exceptions are negligible). They would agree that the
Gospel of the Incarnation is bound up with the particular
historical figure of Jesus: even those who might be in sympathy
with the notion of a " diffused " incarnation in all humanity
would insist on the place of the Person of Jesus, and, indeed,
on that place being at the centre of the good news. To think
about the Gospel and to think about Jesus is really not to have

two thoughts but one. Hence, to talk about incarnation and to leave out this particular historical fact, Jesus, is for the Christian impossible. The theosophist can do it: and it is exactly at that point that we may discern the unbridgeable gulf between Christianity and theosophy. But not all who are at one as to the significance of the particular fact of Jesus are agreed that the Gospel of the Incarnation is bound up so necessarily with that particular fact which we speak of as " The Virgin Birth " that, from the standpoint of dogma, the one is untenable apart from the other. Dr. Gore, despite his firm belief in the Virgin Birth of Christ, was not prepared to go so far as that. Of course he found a dogmatic meaning in the Virgin Birth, but he would not say that a real incarnation necessarily required a Virgin Birth. For those who take this view, the power to separate in thought the Incarnation and the Virgin Birth involves the possibility from the doctrinal standpoint of affirming the Incarnation and not affirming, or even denying, the Virgin Birth.

With regard to the question of authority, for those who do not conceive of any pronouncements of the Church, whether incorporated in Creeds or not, as infallible and, therefore, irreversible, the fact that the Virgin Birth is affirmed in the Creeds raises no different problem from that which already exists in relation to the Bible and to the worship of the Church in general. They would not allow that they were pledged to one way of understanding or interpreting the Creeds, which set up a hard-and-fast distinction between clauses in the Creed, according as they might or might not be interpreted symbolically. Thus, they would regard Gore's attitude as one that represented the outlook of an individual theologian, doubtless very widely held, but possessed of no inherent or exclusive legitimacy.

But it was not only on this subject that Gore was no longer the spokesman of all who claimed the name of Anglo-Catholic, or would have been classed as members of the Anglo-Catholic group. He was far from approving the devotional developments that had grown out of the eucharistic theology which he had always maintained, not least when he was writing the book that gave rise to some misunderstanding, *The Body of Christ* (1901). Those developments had, of course, not been unknown at the beginning of the century, but it was not till much later that they came into prominence. And with regard to them, it would

not be unfair to say that some of those who could not accept
Gore's position in respect of the interpretation of certain
articles of the Creed were willing to go further than he was in
acknowledging as not necessarily illegitimate devotional practices
outside the eucharistic liturgy. The majority of Anglo-Catholics,
who wished to make use of such practices, to have the service
which is known as " Devotions," or, even, in a very few cases,
Benediction, would have agreed with Gore on the credal issue.
But he was no longer in any sense the leader of a party. For
such a role he was, indeed, never properly fitted, nor was it
one to which he aspired. But over a course of many years he
was, even *malgré lui*, in a very real sense the leading theologian
of the Anglo-Catholic movement. That time had passed. His
work was by no means at an end. The achievement of the four
volumes, of which *Belief in God* was the first, was truly remarkable:
even more so, perhaps, the Gifford Lectures on *The Philosophy of
the Good Life* given in 1929-30, so near the end of his life. But
in his work he now stood more definitely apart from the theological as well as from the ecclesiastical tendencies and various
cross-currents of the age than ever before. Yet this isolation
did not react on him in any such way as to induce any in-
definiteness in his conceptions of the nature of Christianity,
of the soundness of the Catholic interpretation of Christianity,
and of the defensibility of the Anglican position.

During this period the Liberal Evangelicals were coming into
increasing prominence within the Church of England. It is,
perhaps, a little difficult to point to any very distinctive feature
of their theology, a fact which has given opportunity of attack
to the upholders of that Evangelical and Protestant tradition of
which, within living memory, such men as J. C. Ryle, Bishop of
Liverpool, Handley Moule, Bishop of Durham, and Prebendary
Webb-Peploe were the protagonists. Those who have followed
most closely in their steps have seen in the Liberal Evangelicals
a deplorable readiness to come to terms with the higher critics
in their attitude to the Bible, and with the Anglo-Catholics in
their ecclesiastical and sacramental conceptions and ceremonial
usages. And to this extent they are right: the Liberal Evangelicals
have abandoned the notion of Biblical inerrancy, just as the
High Churchmen of the *Lux Mundi* period abandoned it. They
have believed themselves to be sacrificing nothing of essential

importance in allowing that the Biblical writers were not exempt from the possibility of mistake in their records. And they have come to lay a stress upon the Church and the sacraments which does involve a certain change of proportion in their attitude to Christian doctrine as compared with that of their fathers in the Evangelical tradition. But the degree of their approximation to Anglo-Catholics in their positive theology may easily be exaggerated. The strength of the latter on the doctrinal side has lain in the closeness of the relation which they have found to exist between the Incarnation and the Church, with its ordered ministry and sacramental system. Modern Anglo-Catholics, conscious of an inadequate appreciation of the theology of atonement in the *Lux Mundi* school and among those who were most under its influence, have deepened the theology of the Anglo-Catholic tradition by connecting it up more closely with the evangelical message of redemption through the Cross.

I am inclined to think that a care for system in theology is much more characteristic of the Anglo-Catholics than of the Liberal Evangelicals. There was a time when Protestant systems stood over against Catholic ones and possessed a similar thoroughness over the whole field of dogma. Such Protestant systems are, of course, still existent, and with the influence of the Barthian school, systematic theology is likely to recover its place within Protestantism. But the suspicion of dogma which grew up in the nineteenth century and left its mark on the theological liberalism of that time has affected the Liberal Evangelicals to a much greater extent than the Anglo-Catholics. As a result, their affiliation, in the sphere of theology, has tended to be much more obviously with those who would definitely be regarded as Anglican Modernists than with the Anglo-Catholics.

In this connexion the position of Dr. E. W. Barnes, Bishop of Birmingham, is specially noteworthy. Some of Dr. Barnes' views and utterances reveal an attitude as remote from that of the Evangelicals of half a century ago as from that of High Churchmen of the same period. But, with the acceptance by Liberal Evangelicals of theories of evolution and of the methods of the higher criticism, and their abandonment of the former notion of the verbal infallibility of the Bible, the difference between them and Dr. Barnes largely disappears. On the other hand, Anglo-Catholics, who would be in agreement with the Bishop on the questions to which I have just referred, would always feel that a wide gulf separated them from him both on the devotional and on the properly theological side. In the volume *Liberal Evangelicalism, An Interpretation*, published in 1923, the final chapter, "The Future of the Evangelical Movement," was contributed by Dr. Barnes, who described himself as "an Evangelical *tout court*." It is interesting to note the words in which he outlines that "modern Evangelicalism" with which he affirmed the future to lie. It is not to be assumed that all his collaborators in the book, or all who to-day would call themselves Liberal Evangelicals, would be in wholehearted agreement with his statement. But a comparison between it and the kind of brief presentation of the Gospel which Evangelicals of an older school would have given and would still give is of great interest. He writes as follows:

"We go back to the Gospel and take as our basis the ethical and spiritual Revelation of Christ. We rest on the sure and certain conviction that that Revelation will justify itself by its appeal to all that is finest in human nature. Christ, we affirm, had the words of Eternal Life. . . . His teaching as to the nature of God, as to man's duty and destiny, we confidently affirm to be the truth. On the Gospel we build the Christian faith. This, we maintain, is the old Evangelical position. We seek to convert men, to turn them to Christ, to persuade them to follow His example, to obey His precepts, to see in the power of His Holy Spirit the only hope of the regeneration of mankind. So will men love Him and know Him to be both Lord and Saviour. All else in Christian worship and dogma is subsidiary to this. Much of it is important, but compared with the central nucleus of our faith, as we have just stated it, it hardly matters."

Up to the end of the last century, and, indeed, in the first decade of this one, such a statement of faith would have come quite naturally from a Broad or Liberal Churchman, but hardly from an Evangelical. Its inclusion in a volume intended to be representative of what was believed by Evangelicals, even though the noun was qualified by the adjective "Liberal," shows how considerable had been the influence of those associations of Evangelicals which came into existence about the year 1908, and were then known as "The Groups." From that beginning has derived the association of Liberal Evangelicals familiar as the Anglican Evangelical Group Movement, with which many of the present English Bishops have been connected. But while the importance and the influence of this Movement continue to be considerable, it has not contributed as much to the study of the problems of theology as have the Anglo-Catholics, the Modernists who descend from the old Broad Church school and not from the Evangelicals, and those scholars who represent an Anglicanism in front of which it would be inaccurate to add any descriptive adjective. The Liberal Evangelicals have not produced any joint work which, as a constructive treatment of the subject-matter of Christian theology, can be set alongside of *Lux Mundi* or of *Essays Catholic and Critical*. Nor have those notable books, to which anyone seriously interested in the great Christian doctrines and their expositions by individual scholars would turn, come from members of that group. I have in mind such studies as *God in Christian Thought and Experience* by Dr. W. R. Matthews, *The Incarnate Lord* by Father Lionel Thornton, *The Idea of Atonement in Christian Theology* by the late Dr. Hastings Rashdall, and *The Christian Sacraments* by the late Dr. O. C. Quick. The same is true if one thinks of the Anglicans who are specially to the fore in connexion with the philosophy of religion, Dr. William Temple, Dr. C. C. J. Webb, Professor A. E. Taylor, and Dr. Matthews. There would be an important reservation to make had Canon V. F. Storr continued to make large contributions to that field of research in which both metaphysics and theology have so deep an interest. More rightly than anyone else could he be called the leader of the Liberal Evangelicals. But he withdrew from that field, at least so far as published work is concerned.

The situation is interesting enough to deserve a little more exploration. A growing party or group, be its sphere what it may, religious, political, artistic, is likely, especially if it is conscious of meeting a need that no other group can meet with any equal adequacy, to make its principles widely known through the written word. That word may be of many kinds, and may include the ephemeral pamphlet along with the profound study in which its message is expounded and defended and shown in all its various relationships. How much Barthianism has gained by the presentation of its conception of Christianity in the Biblical and theological writings which have come from Barth and others is obvious enough. Nothing at all similar has happened in the case of the Liberal Evangelicals. That English religious movements do not run on the same lines as those which proceed from Germany is true, but does not explain this particular difference, since the Anglo-Catholics have in joint volumes and individual writings made their theological position quite plain.

I would suggest that the Liberal Evangelicals have been confronted with a special difficulty, which largely accounts for the comparative absence of treatises expressive of their point of view. The older Evangelicalism, in its opposition to Roman Catholic theology and to that of the Tractarians and their successors, relied on two principal doctrines, the infallibility and all-sufficiency of Holy Scripture, and the Atonement viewed as a penal substitutionary sacrifice: this latter was the objective truth of which the doctrine of justification by faith only was the subjective counterpart. In strict dogmatic order every other doctrine was, for the older Evangelicalism, secondary to these. But neither of these foundation-principles remained unchanged for the Liberal Evangelicals. However carefully they stated their willingness to accept the results of a sane and reverent criticism, there could be no doubt that they had abandoned the earlier position. The kind of appeal to every word of Scripture which was possible for their predecessors was not possible for them. As to the Atonement, while the difference is not so clear, and many of the Liberal group have doubtless been substantially at one with the others in their interpretation of the redeeming work of Christ, the rigidity of the past has gone. Let anyone read the essay on " The Work of Christ " by R. T. Howard, now Provost of Coventry, in *Liberal Evangelicalism* (1923) or the volume entitled *The Atonement in History and Life* (1929) to which a number of scholars broadly classifiable as Liberal Evangelicals contributed, and he will be struck by the change of tone, if he is at all acquainted with earlier expositions written from the Evangelical standpoint. The latter book is specially significant, since, as Dr. Wilson, Bishop of Chelmsford, remarks in the foreword, no one who was a " thorough-going ' Subjectivist ' " was included. But there is no idea that Evangelicalism is committed to one orthodox interpretation of what the Atonement means, and that the doctrine of penal substitution. Now, if Christianity is no longer bound up, as undoubtedly the older Evangelicals thought that it was bound up, with these two dogmatic affirmations, the theological position of the heirs to the evangelical tradition, who have given up its rigidity in these two matters, is less obviously distinguishable from that of other groups than was once the case.

If we look at the whole theological situation, with an eye to the historic differences that have found a place within the Church of England, we may note two contrary tendencies. On the one hand, those differences persist and, at their extremes, have become sharper and more irreconcilable. There is a section of Anglo-Catholics whose theology is decisively Roman Catholic rather than Anglican. There are points where they might withhold full agreement with the Roman Catholic Church in its devotional and disciplinary system; but, broadly speaking, they see in that Church the upholder and expositor of Catholic truth, and would desire to affirm the full agreement of the Church of England in its theology with the Church of Rome. This group has, in effect, arrived at the position taken up by W. G. Ward at the end of his Anglican days. For it, the idea of an *Anglican* theology is intolerable. Secondly, the conservative Evangelicals, as represented, for instance, by the Bible Churchmen's Missionary Society, regard the theology of evangelical Protestantism, without any infiltration from the side either of the High Church or of the Broad Church, as the only dogmatic system that has a true, historic, legal, and doctrinal right to exist within the Church of England. There would, probably, be divisions of opinion as to how far the Caroline school of High Churchmen might fairly be allowed to come within the four corners of the Church of England. It is doubtful, indeed, whether anyone would go so far as to contend that such men as Andrewes and Cosin and Bramhall had no proper right to be within the Church of England at all. Certainly Dr. Wace, who was a conservative Evangelical and a very strong Protestant, would not have said so. But it would not be admitted that such divines most truly represented the mind of the Church of England, and the doctrinal positions characteristic of the Tractarians and the later Anglo-Catholics would be condemned as definitely alien. The same judgment would be passed upon the Modernists.

Thus we see the extremes of the High Church and the Evangelical groups not only in the straightest opposition to one another, but claiming in either case that they and they alone are in the true and full sense capable of expressing the mind and of expounding the theology of the Church of England. No such claim is made from the extremity of the Broad Church wing; but with some of the presentations of modernist teaching it is probable that not only the extreme sections of other groups but a great mass of central opinion finds itself far more out of touch than used to be the case with the Broad Churchmanship of Victorian days. The break with the historic Christian tradition in matters of doctrine appears to be much more radical than if it were just an affair of liberty of judgment claimed in relation to particular Biblical narratives or articles of the Creed. How far such an impression of a radical break would be accepted as a fact is a question which, if pressed to its ultimate issue, would raise the whole problem of the relation of form to substance in the Christian tradition, which, as we have seen, was debated in the exchange of letters between Dr. Sanday and N. P. Williams, then a Fellow of Exeter College, Oxford. It is, perhaps, in Christology that the problem is most acute. Any re-statement which is essentially incompatible with the faith that Jesus Christ is both truly God and truly man involves a break not only with the form but also with the substance of historic Christianity.

It was the belief that some of the opinions voiced at the Girton Conference of Modern Churchmen in 1921 were incompatible with that faith which led to the protests that followed upon that Conference. It was held that those opinions did not cohere with the teaching of St. Paul in Phil. ii. 5-11, and with that of St. John in the Prologue to the fourth Gospel. One of the foremost figures of the Conference was the late Dr. Rashdall, Dean of Carlisle. He read a paper at Girton, and afterwards, in a sermon preached in Carlisle Cathedral, defended the position he had taken up. In the course of it he gave careful expression to his conception of what is or should be meant when Christ is affirmed to be divine. " We can form," he said, " no higher conception of God than we see exhibited in humanity at its highest, and in Christ, as in no other man before or since, we may see what humanity at its highest is; and therefore in Him we believe that God has made a full and sufficient revelation of Himself. His character is the character of God. In Him God is once and for all revealed." That this was an adequate rendering of the twin doctrines of Christ's divinity and His incarnation, as they had been expounded by St. Paul and St. John, and as they had been formulated at Nicæa in the Creed and at Chalcedon in the Definition, was what the critics of Dr. Rashdall and of the other pronouncements made at Girton could not allow.

With the interpretation given by Dr. Rashdall in 1921 may be compared that of the Rev. R. D. Richardson in his paper on " The Significance of Jesus for Faith," read at the Modern Churchmen's Conference in 1936. After explaining his doubt-fulness as to Professor Dodd's phrase with regard to Christ that He " entered decisively into history," as suggesting overmuch that the world is one into which " God comes only from with-out," he proceeded to say that " we now think of the universe as being the result of a continuous process in which God energizes continuously. Yet the fact remains that there are at times fuller emergencies into history of the Divine Spirit, and that Jesus is a decisive revelation of the character and Will of God." He affirmed that the word " Incarnation," if the notion of a miraculous conception was eliminated from it, " alone conveys the essential thought of the uniqueness of Jesus. Again, we modern Christians see the same significance in Jesus as led our fore-fathers to speak of Him as the God-Man and to formulate the doctrine of the Trinity, although the valuation of Jesus in terms of religious experience now leads thinkers to find the old theolog-ical formulations of these doctrines unsatisfying. Let it then suffice for me to say that here was One Who was truly man; Who was able so to live and talk, and be ' to the Eternal Goodness what his right hand is to a man,' as the *Theologia Germanica* says, that His life presents a series of Epiphanies— glorious unveilings of God."

I have quoted at some length, since Mr. Richardson's words show very clearly the meaning which one modern Churchman, who may not speak for all, but may not improperly be supposed to speak for many, of those associated with him in the Modern Churchmen's Union, attaches to the doctrine of the Incarnation. That the language differs from that which is natural to Evangelicals and Anglo-Catholics is obvious: as to the substance of the thought it is anyhow doubtful whether there is real identity between the belief expressed in the quotation and that which would be shared by the above-mentioned groups. Those who do not recognize such identity would feel estranged from the theology presented to them, in the same way as the extremes of Anglo-Catholicism and Evangelical Protestantism feel estranged from one another in respect of their doctrinal positions.

Theological differences within the Church of England have sharpened. But that is only one part of the story. In contrast to this tendency there is another which makes for an abatement of strife, a concentration upon those fundamental beliefs in which the religion of the Gospel has been given doctrinal expression, and a readiness both to be content with diversity where beliefs of that order are not involved, and to consider anew the nature of such diversity. Men do not always differ as much as they think they do; that applies to theologians as well as to the rest of mankind, and it is possible to overestimate through long convention both the depth and the significance o theological disagreements. Nor should it be forgotten that such disagreements are often, to a great extent, the result of a difference in emphasis. That was partly true of the Christological controversies in the ancient Church. The stress fell either on the Godhead or on the manhood of Christ. Each stress was in itself legitimate, for since Christ is both God and man, no exception can be taken to the theologian who draws out, with particular attention and care, what is the meaning and what is the outcome of either of these great truths. It was only when the interest of the theologian or of the school was focussed on the particular truth in such a way that the reality of the other, equally necessary, truth was obscured, that the danger of what might properly be called heresy became real. Or let another instance be given which is more pertinent in relation to the history of the Church of England from the sixteenth century onwards. The reality of justification by faith and the reality of sacramental grace stand in no essential antithesis to one another, but it is natural that one Christian should emphasize the former, another the latter. So far there is no occasion for dispute. But if either doctrine be treated as though the other did not rightfully exist, then it is inevitable that such acute controversy will arise as will lead many to suppose that a choice must be made between the two. Thus, an unreal contrast will be set up, and the doctrines will appear to confront one another as alternatives.

The unitive tendency in theology within the Church of England

is marked by a reaction against the one-sided emphases which
have been productive of so much violent argument and constant
misunderstandings. It is a tendency which has been greatly
helped by the presence within the Church of theologians whose
natural approach to the problems of theology is not from one
side or another of the group divisions, but from a detached
position in which they have been content to be Anglicans.
They have had their leanings and preferences; but their effort
has been—and it has been one so natural to them that it has not
been a consciously contrived effort—to expound theological
truth as men who know that such truth is no peculiar property
of the Church of England, while, at the same time, it is from
within the Church of England, and as inheritors of a traditional
atmosphere and method which is native to the Church of England
and to no other Christian body, that they have brought their
labours of exposition and interpretation to fulfilment.   Of
theologians no longer with us I have in mind such men as
Maurice and Hort, Lightfoot and Frederick Temple, Church
and Swete. With them may rightly be classed, among more
recent divines, Dr. A. C. Headlam, Dr. O. C. Quick, R. H.
Malden, Dean of Wells, and Dr. S. C. Carpenter, Dean of Exeter.
In all these cases, and in others which a reader may feel appropriate to add to their number, there is a theological temper
which is both Catholic and Evangelical, and at the same time
inherently Anglican. It appears also in men who are more
generally regarded as High Churchmen or as Evangelicals than
as Anglicans without any distinguishing prefix. It is a temper
that can be recognized in the work of Gore, though it was not
one of his most striking characteristics; and to its presence
in T. W. Drury, who, before his successive episcopates, first
over the see of Sodor and Man, and then at Ripon, was Principal
of Ridley Hall, is largely due the fact that he won a special
measure of trust and respect throughout the Church of England.
In its more particular bearing on the problems of theology
this temper reveals itself in an intellectual attitude and method
of approach of which some notice must be taken.

The Church of England, since the Reformation, cannot
claim to have produced through its ministers a *Summa Theologica*
which can be compared to the works of Aquinas and Calvin,
or of many other, if less famous, names to be found on the

roll of Roman Catholic and Protestant divines. The nearest approach thereto is that celebrated study of Church doctrine and practice, *The Laws of Ecclesiastical Polity*, of which Richard Hooker was the author. But that was not, in its proper nature, the full exposition of a theological system. It took its origin in the particular and passing controversies of the age; and while Hooker's judicious temper and comprehensive outlook elevated his work to a position of lasting importance as a theological classic which cannot be treated as of merely antiquarian significance, it is not a work of theological reference after the manner of the writings of Luther and the sermons of John Wesley. These form a ground of appeal and almost a standard of orthodoxy for Lutherans and Methodists respectively. If nothing of that kind is true for Hooker's *Laws*, still less is it true for any other theological book that has appeared from within the Church of England.

But one thing Hooker did of the greatest importance, though the value of it may be differently estimated. He did, in effect, distinguish between doctrines of the first and the second order of importance. That is, he did not treat of Christian theology as though it were a chain whose strength could be measured by that of its weakest links. The nature of his treatise, of course, makes it necessary to avoid confident assertions; had he been engaged on a systematic work such as Calvin produced in his *Institutes*, one might receive a different impression. Yet it is difficult to imagine that in such a work he would have expounded a precise doctrine of grace or of predestination or of the eucharist, as the one that carried with it the full authority of the Church. It is this attitude of restraint which has continued to be one of the marks of Anglican theology and gives it a peculiar colour. To this is due the fact that, along with sharp divisions of theological opinion which have at times appeared to dominate the Anglican scene, there has been a central body of Anglicanism which neither of the opposing groups has been able to dominate, a body with which the final responsibility for a theological lead has rested. To those who distrust mediating theological tendencies this characteristic of theological Anglicanism can be irritating and vexatious in a high degree. It can convey the impression of shirking rather than of taking responsibility. But whatever be thought of it, there can be no doubt of its persistence and of its success. So far as the signs of the times enable a forecast to be made, I should anticipate an increase of this tendency. It is one that is likely to result in such a mutual approach to one another of Liberal Anglo-Catholicism and Liberal Evangelicalism as will lead to the vanishing of the acuter points of divergence which still remain. This could not happen if it were not that these two groups are themselves looking for a more central position within the Church of England. In respect of Anglicanism their movement is centripetal, not centrifugal: and at the centre they meet with a well-established theological Anglicanism.

An explanation of these facts, in so far as they are accepted as correctly stated, might appear to reside in the ecclesiastical position of the Church of England. The distinctiveness in its theology would be viewed by some observers as the natural by-product of the isolation of its life. Because the Church of England as an institution does not cohere with any other Christian body, so, it might be argued, its doctrinal outlook conforms to no recognized type of Christian theology. Such an account would not be wholly false. Indeed, the very important introduction prefixed by Dr. Headlam to his book *The Church of England* (1924), which incorporates the charge he delivered in his diocese, shows how much can be said for such an estimate. The opening words, " The Church of England occupies a somewhat special place among the different branches of the Christian Church," prepare us for the description of its characteristics which follows. It is obvious, unless the Bishop has entirely misjudged the actual situation, that the life and religion of the Church of England cannot be made to square with fixed presuppositions as to the appearance which a truly Christian Church should present. The different views taken of it, to which he draws attention, supply sufficient proof of this conclusion.

But to say that is not at all to say that theologians of the Church of England are concerned to expound a brand of theology which is simply the reflexion of the " special place " which that Church occupies. Such an idea, if entertained, would mean that the appeal of the Church of England at the time of the Reformation to the standards of the primitive Church, and not least to those standards in their theological content and implication, had been overlooked. Anglican divines undoubtedly held that the medieval Church had gone astray from those norms which a study of the theology of the early Christian centuries revealed. But it was not their desire to erect a system of all-inclusive belief which would rival the great systems, which, on the one hand, the Schoolmen, on the other Calvin and later Protestant theologians, both Lutheran and Reformed, had elaborated as the only true accounts that could be given of Christianity on its intellectual side. Accordingly the work done by Anglican theologians has never compared with that of other communions as a systematic exposition of Christian doctrine. In attention to particular subjects there has been no lack of Anglican scholarship, and that of the first order of competence. Such an exposition of Christology in its historical setting as Bishop Bull's *Defence of the Nicene Creed* is a famous example, and it won recognition beyond the borders of the Church of England.

It is from this historical background that we may best approach the work of Anglican theologians during the last thirty years. The first war and its consequences had meant both a stirring and a confusing of thought. The most fundamental questions of metaphysics and theology came almost spontaneously into the foreground. And in so far as they were, whether consciously or by implication, addressed to the Christian Church, they might be summed up in two major enquiries: first, what has the Church to say about the relation of God to the world? secondly, what has the Church to say about the relation of Christian doctrine to modern thought? These enquiries were not, of course, in any way new: but they were charged with a new intensity because of the vast perplexity, taking different forms but all springing from a common root of intellectual bewilderment, which had spread over the minds of people who had lived through the undermining of material security. To many it seemed as though the Christian Creed were discredited by the events which showed how unsubstantial and fleeting had been those dreams of steady progress in civilization which the generation before the war had come near to investing with the nature of reality.

This widespread bewilderment was intensified by the appearance of a new factor in the intellectual field. The new psychology had taken its rise about 1895, and by the end of the first world-war was showing itself a force to be reckoned with. It made far-reaching claims for its method, and asserted that it had reached conclusions of the first importance for religion. These conclusions or supposed conclusions of psychological research present to the Christian theologian or apologist a problem more difficult, because more subtle and elusive, than any that arose out of the conclusions which the Darwinian biologists reached. In the older controversy it was the framework of man's existence as a moral and spiritual being that was under review. What was asserted and denied related to the connexion of man, in respect of his bodily structure, with the animal creation. But a belief in biological evolution did not necessarily rule out teleology; it did not logically involve a theory of mind as a by-product of matter, of psychophysical parallelism, and of blind, mechanical process. A naturalistic philosophy, ruling out freedom, God, and immortality, was not the true offspring of the Darwinian view of the *Origin of Species*, however true it is that there were scientists and theologians who believed this to be the case. It would hardly be going too far to say that Darwin left all the old and great problems belonging to the philosophy of religion just where he found them: nor did he make any claim to have done anything more cheering or more alarming.

It is otherwise with psychology, in so far as its subject-matter goes. For as a science it is concerned with man in his actual life, mental, spiritual, æsthetic, moral. It cannot, indeed, directly challenge the truth of what a man believes, or the transcendental character of a moral law to which he yields his obedience. But it does claim to throw light on the inner movements and impulses which are at work in the man who believes and obeys. And the conclusions which have been drawn are, in some instances, utterly adverse to any affirmation of religious reality. The whole position is excellently summed up by Dr. Grensted in his Bampton Lectures entitled *Psychology and God* (1930):

" It is," he says, " only in the field of psychology that there is still a living problem. For the psychologist studies not only external facts, but the very processes of the mind which perceive them and estimate their worth. And

---

* Between these points a page of the manuscript is missing. I have given in my own words what was evidently the gist of it.—EDITOR.

if he shows, as sometimes he claims to show, that religion is simply a natural by-product of these processes, having no validity beyond the processes themselves, then indeed man walketh in a vain shadow, and the shadow is his own."

The forms which the psychological threat to religion takes are considered and criticized by Dr. Grensted in his Lectures. The task to which he and other Christian students of psychology have set themselves is as important as was that which was undertaken in the course of the controversy about evolution. But a great difference in standpoint and method is immediately observable.

Sixty or seventy years ago the question seemed to be primarily one not of interpretation but of fact. It was any actual relationship between man, in his bodily structure, and the lower animals that Christian apologists denied. Canon Storr in his work, *The Development of English Theology in the Nineteenth Century* (1913), which carries us as far as 1860 and leaves the Darwinian disputes practically untouched, nevertheless indicates the attitude which seems to him to have been common in the Church of England, when he refers to Baden Powell, one of the contributors to *Essays and Reviews*, as " one of the very few theologians who were imbued with a scientific spirit and were friendly to science," and notes that he extended " a warm welcome to the evolutionary hypothesis." Bishop Samuel Wilberforce, with his jeering remark at the meeting of the British Association, and Disraeli, avowing himself to be on the side of the angels, were more typical of current Church opinion. It took time for this early impression of the irreconcilability of the whole Darwinian position with the Christian doctrine of man to be removed; and it is, of course, still true that any teaching which affirms an inheritance in man derived from the lower mammals is in some quarters denounced as essentially un-Christian. But, broadly speaking, the centre of controversy has shifted from the problem of fact to the problem of the interpretation of fact. And there are many scientists who would affirm with as great assurance as any theologian that there is no single article in the creed of Theism or of Christianity which is imperilled by the Darwinian theory. The issues raised as a result of psychological enquiry have not centred in one particular question, nor have they been so clear cut as to allow of any spectacular contrast of scientist and theologian. Nor has any single psychologist,

not Freud nor Jung nor any other, shown signs of gaining through
his researches and the conclusions to which they have led a
position comparable to that which would now be very generally
assigned to Darwin. Some may make this claim for Freud, but
they represent a particular school, not the whole body of students
of psychology.

So far it might seem as though Christian thinkers who have
paid special attention to developments in psychology, and have
displayed a calmness not so characteristic of their predecessors,
might view the situation with contentment. And so they might,
if it were just a matter of defending the chief Christian affirmations as to man's spiritual nature against direct assault, or against
the negative conclusions directly involved in the teaching of the
Behaviourist and the Freudian schools. But the real danger
is far less easy to meet: it would probably be near the mark to
say that it consists principally in the impression of insecurity
in the foundations of religion which has been conveyed through
psychological teaching and writing: the comparative study of
religion has to some extent tended to produce a like effect.

The Christian psychologist, or the Christian interpreter of
the varied religious history of mankind, has his own problems
to survey and his specialized contributions to make. Dr. Grensted
and Dr. Selbie, Dr. C. C. J. Webb and Dr. Harold Smith are
among those who have laboured in these fields. But a good deal
of the best work in theology during the last generation has
come from the pen of the constructive philosopher or theologian rather than from that of the purposeful apologist. For
unfavourable though some might judge the present age to be
for systematic work in the grand style, difficult though it may
be to imagine the appearance of a new *Summa Theologica*, it is,
nevertheless, true that Christian thinkers are applying themselves
with increasing confidence to work that both illuminates the
essential character of the Gospel and reveals the bearing of the
Gospel upon the deepest problems of thought and life. It is
with this task, and with some of those who have specially devoted
themselves to it, that we shall now be concerned.

Let this be said, first, by way of introduction. Theologians
of the Church of England (and I think that the same is, broadly
speaking, the case with English and Scottish divines belonging
to other communions) have combined a regard for secular

philosophy with an unwillingness to pledge themselves to the
support of any one philosophical system. Hooker and Butler did
not assign to any of the great masters of philosophy the position
given by St. Thomas Aquinas to Aristotle, nor must the title
" The Cambridge Platonists " be taken too seriously. Again,
German theologians have tended to be more sensitive towards,
and more influenced by, contemporaneous movements in philosophy than have their English contemporaries. There is no parallel
in Great Britain to the stir which the Hegelian metaphysic
produced in German theological circles, to the flow and ebbing
and cross-currents in religious thought for which Hegel was
responsible. On the other hand, in typical English theology
there has been no such violent reaction against any possibility
of philosophy mediating some knowledge of God, such as we
associate with the Barthian school. In consequence the attitude
of this theology to the whole field of metaphysical enquiry
has been more detached and equable than has been the theology
of Germany. It has had no prejudice against the confidence
of philosophers in reason, as a trustworthy weapon which can
take man some way into the secrets of the universe. But the
habitual English preference for the historic and the concrete
over the speculative and the abstract is a powerful incentive
to a stress upon the revelation of which the Bible is the record.
The general result of this is that in the work of, anyhow, the
most competent English theologians a certain comprehensive
spirit is to be marked which can make itself at home in the
fields alike of Biblical, of dogmatic, and of philosophical
exposition. The obvious danger is that of a superficial amateurishness, and not all English theology has escaped that peril.
But it may not be a worse fault than that of a narrow and
unimaginative specialism, and from the one as from the other the
theologians who are of the front rank have kept themselves free.

The most influential exponents within the Church of England
of a theology which is continuously sensitive to philosophical
enquiries were, probably, Dr. William Temple, Dr. Matthews,
the Dean of St. Paul's, and Dr. O. C. Quick, who became
Regius Professor of Divinity at Oxford. If I were attempting
to enumerate all the books of importance which have been written
by Anglicans in relation to philosophical theology, the task
would take me too far afield. Such *magna opera* as Dr. Tennant's

Philosophical Theology (1928-30) and Professor A. E. Taylor's *The Faith of a Moralist* (1930) could not be passed over. But the reason for the particular selection which I have made above lies in the continuous teaching, bearing upon ultimate questions as to the relation of God to the world, which these thinkers have been giving. A small library of nine books would suffice for a very thorough grounding in philosophy of religion and dogmatics. A cast-away upon a desert island would find most of his needs met had he been able to save from his ship the following volumes: by Dr. Temple, *Mens Creatrix* (1917), *Christus Veritas* (1924), and *Nature, Man and God* (1934); by Dr. Matthews, *God in Christian Thought and Experience* (1930), *Essays in Construction* (1933), and *The Purpose of God* (1935); by Dr. Quick, *The Ground of Faith and the Chaos of Thought* (1931), *The Christian Sacraments* (1927), and *Doctrines of the Creed* (1938). He would through the study of them gain both a clear understanding of the main positions which Christian theology has always been resolute to affirm in respect of the nature of the universe and of man's place therein, and also a safeguard against a sceptical pessimism arising out of the uneasy position in which he was finding himself.

A survey of these works would disclose points at which their eminent authors were in imperfect agreement with one another. But that fact is of no present relevance as compared with the firm conviction which they all share that Christian theology is a rational system of thought, and can be expounded and defended in this its true nature. In their reactions from other traditions in doctrine they would vary to some extent among themselves; but they are united in their presentation of a philosophical theology, whereof the proper home is the Church of England, and not the Roman Catholic Church, nor the Barthian fortress, nor the groves of Liberal Protestantism. Further, as against the unsystematic character of modern philosophy, to which Dr. Matthews, in particular, has called attention, these thinkers are confident that Christian theology has an answer of metaphysical relevance which points the way out of these discordant and chaotic tendencies. It may be an unsensational method both of theology and of apologetic which is thus employed for the expression and vindication of Christian truth, but it has the great value of freedom from anything of the nature of undue attention to present needs, however pressing they may seem. The greatest theological tradition of Christianity has laid stress upon the possibility and necessity of rational thinking. To this these Anglican theologians remain faithful: they take note of all that is going on in the thinking of their age; they know that the artists and the physicists have things to say which matter, as well as the professional philosophers. But they refuse to be intimidated by new fashions, from whatever quarter they may come. They are, obviously, first hand in their judgments and in their criticisms. No one could read and ponder the pages in which, in *The Ground of Faith and the Chaos of Thought*, Dr. Quick outlines the teaching of Professor Whitehead and Sir James Jeans as to the nature of physical reality, and then passes to a discussion of their metaphysical cosmology and their idea of God, without realizing that here was a Christian theologian displaying in a high degree gifts of appreciation and criticism, whereby the whole problem is made more intelligible and the way opened for a solution of it which could not, without culpable superficiality, be ignored. The same may be said of Dr. Matthews' examination of the teleological question, not least of his criticism of the attempt to substitute a belief in emergent evolution, that is, of an immanent teleology, for one that is based upon the belief in Creative Mind. As for Dr. Temple, he is the constructive Christian philosopher, with a comprehensiveness of outlook and a mastery of the art of exposition such as is very rarely met.

No writer will lightly take upon himself the task of appraising the work of his contemporaries. Especially when it is men of thought rather than of action whom he surveys, he will do well to remember that the only human verdict that really matters is the one that he cannot write, since he is of the present, not of the future. But it is not with the excellencies and limitations of particular theologians of to-day that I am concerned, but with movements and tendencies which, whatever may some day be said of them, have a special significance and importance in this age. The confidence which is to be seen in the work of those of whom I have written is a fact full of encouragement. At a time when a deep pessimism as to human life and human civilization is showing itself, and can point to much that justifies its negative conclusions, it is one of the brightest signs in the intellectual sky that Christian thinkers are fearlessly proclaiming the service to truth, and through truth to life, which Christian theology in its great affirmations about God and about man can and does render. A further pointer in that direction is to be seen in the volume edited in 1939 by the Bishop of Oxford, and incorporating the work of a number of scholars of high reputation, entitled *The Study of Theology*. The only sufficient corrective of bad theology is good theology; the only antidote to an uninstructed and self-confident amateurishness is to be found in the professional competence which remains both humble and human. Such a book as *The Study of Theology* has the value of showing the nature of the country and the importance of the discoveries that are to be made in it.

In the Free Churches too the tendency is the same. The older Protestantism, as it was represented in English Nonconformity, had a deep interest in systematic theology. A tradition that owed itself so much to Calvin could not fail to do so. But for several reasons the first decade of this century was not favourable, in its religious atmosphere, to the production of works of high dogmatic importance from within the Free Churches. It was, indeed, a constant theme with Dr. Forsyth that it was the stress that he laid upon theology which was the root-cause of the bewilderment and sense of strangeness occasioned by his writings. It is certain that he was near to regarding himself as a *Vox clamantis*. The situation is very different today. That is probably due in part to the impressiveness of Forsyth's own work. So profound a theologian may not meet with due recognition during his lifetime, though in his latter days his name came to be held in great honour as that of one of the masters in theology. But it may be that his influence has been wider and more marked after his death. The circumstances of the world from which he passed in 1922 have been such as to underline the truth of his message, and to reveal him as one who anticipated the returning insistence upon the place of theology. As Dr. Whale writes in his " Foreword " to *The Work of Christ*, which is Forsyth's most systematic study of the doctrine of the Atonement, and has recently been reprinted:

" He knew that an undogmatic Christianity was a contradiction in terms. So far from being out of date, his work anticipates by nearly a quarter of a century the ' realism ' of our modern theology, without the extravagances into which it has been led by the excessive logic of Barth. . . . The marrow of a truly modern divinity is here for all who will feed on it."

The Free Churches, hardly less than the Church of England, have had their attention directed to the grounds, nature, and affirmations of Christian theology by the Faith and Order Movement. Whatever the limitations or actual defects of that Movement, it has the great merit of calling for a real and comprehensive theology, and from the beginnings it has been clear that it could make no headway apart from a firm hold upon the historic Christian doctrine of God and Christ, which had been affirmed in the undivided ancient Church, and reaffirmed, at the time of the Reformation, by the Protestant communions, with the exception of the Socinians. Thus it was stated at the Lausanne Conference of 1927, in the Report of Section IV, which the full Conference received, *nemine contradicente*, that:

" Notwithstanding the differences in doctrine among us, we are united in a common Christian Faith which is proclaimed in the Holy Scriptures, and is witnessed to and safeguarded in the Œcumenical Creed, commonly called the Nicene, and in the Apostles' Creed, which Faith is continuously confirmed in the spiritual experience of the Church of Christ."

One of the British theologians most closely associated with the Movement has been Dr. A. E. Garvie. A Congregationalist like his friend Forsyth, his natural tendencies in theology have been in certain respects very different. Forsyth passed through and out of a period of theological Liberalism, and his reaction against that type of religious thought was too sharp for him to be quite able to do justice to its positive merits. Dr. Garvie has stood consistently on the liberal side (his aversion from Barthianism is one instance thereof), but it is with a liberal orthodoxy that his mind has been in harmony. And it is not, I think, unjust to him to suggest that the great share he has taken in the Movement towards Christian Unity has not only enriched his spiritual life, but also given him a fuller appreciation of the positive values of dogmatic theology.

Dr. Garvie has set forth his systematic, or, as he prefers to call it, " Constructive Theology " in three large volumes, which bear the names of *The Christian Doctrine of the Godhead*, *The Christian Ideal for Human Society*, and *The Christian Belief in God*, and cover the years 1925 to 1933. The last, which is philosophical and apologetic, is, as he remarks in his preface, the first in order. They represent the need which a very independent-minded theologian, who does not easily align himself with any one tradition, feels for a comprehensive Christian theology that will be true to its own foundations and be capable of meeting the problems that arise in connexion with man's history, both secular and more narrowly religious, and with the metaphysical theories whereby man has tried to give a rational account of the universe.

CHAPTER IV

THE SCOTTISH TRADITION

TO turn from England to Scotland and to view the theological scene as it reveals itself in the northern country through the movement of the years is to become aware at once of a difference of the first importance. In England theological developments have had their place within a changing ecclesiastical picture. That is clearest if attention is concentrated upon the Church of England. Particular theological stresses and tendencies have gained their significance, not, usually, as the expressions of the teaching of an individual scholar, but as characteristic of a group which saw in them the dogmatic emphasis that cohered with its whole conception of Christian life, thought, and devotion. Theological movement in England has been continually involved in controversies that have ranged far afield, and raised questions which have, at least apparently, concerned themselves not so much with whether such and such opinions were true, but whether they ought to be held and taught in the Church of England. There is no ground here for any cynical suggestion that truth was given a place of subordinate importance. But the situation in the Church of England, in view of past history, of the traditions preserved within it and gaining support, at this point from the Prayer Book, at that from the Articles, of its relation to State and Nation as the national Church, yet not as though State or Nation had created it—all these circumstances, with the consequences derived from them, have greatly affected the way in which theological problems have been approached and discussed, and have been responsible for the peculiar degree of interest which some problems, such as those connected with eucharistic doctrine, have stirred.

Of this no evidence more convincing could be provided than that which the controversies over Prayer Book Revision and the debates in Parliament furnish. It is improbable that anything similar could have taken place in any other country. Certainly the explanation is not to be found in a special flair of the English-man for theological disputation. It is continually being made clear that the Englishman's general attitude is one of aloofness if not of aversion: it is not easy to bring him to understand that theological affirmations and denials are concerned with what is not irrelevant to himself, namely the meaning of his own existence and of the world which he inhabits. Nor can it be said that those who were opposed to the revision in the form it had taken were all Evangelical Churchmen, who saw in what was proposed a threat to the true doctrines of grace as held by those English Reformers who owed not a little to Luther, but much more to Calvin. There were many whose antipathy to the measures was not based on anything much more definite than on the belief that alterations were to be made which would lessen the cleavage that separated the Church of England from the Church of Rome. Yet, at point after point, the justification for such an attitude could be found only in a theology that had reached definite conclusions as to the nature of dogma, as to grace and faith, as to the Church and its authority, and, if Barth is to be followed in his systematic theology and in other writings, on the meaning of the Word of God, and the legitimacy of the *analogia entis* as an argument leading from man to God.

The position of the Free Churches in England is obviously different. But they too are not impervious to the pressure of the English and Anglican atmosphere. That was, I think, apparent in the case of so great a theologian as Dr. Forsyth. He and others could not regard themselves simply as detached observers, quite external to Anglican controversies. All non-Roman Catholic communions in England are related to one another by reason of their common derivation, in the forms which they possess, from the events of the sixteenth century prolonged into the seventeenth. The dogmatic differences are unintelligible apart from those events, and those events do not belong to the historical past, as though then and there they had come to a final settlement. The theologian was likely to find himself compelled to be a controversialist and an apologist, taking account of much that was of an accidental rather than of a substantial character in its relation to theology proper.

Markedly different, so far as I can judge, has been the situation in Scotland. The nature of the theological tradition in Scottish

Presbyterianism has been unmistakable, and has not been the subject of controversial discussion as a ground of debate within the Church. The High Church movement there, if the phrase be appropriate, has aimed at a recovery and a clearer exposition of a sacramental side of Church life as part of the legitimate heritage, never repudiated, which links the Church of to-day with the Church in all ages. On the other hand, there has been no equivalent interest in the recovery of episcopacy, for the simple reason that the presbyter has been conceived of as endowed with the powers of the primitive *episcopus*.

Two great debates, and only two, have divided Scottish Churchmen in the last century. The first has referred to questions concerning establishment, and takes its start in the events that led to the disruption of 1843. It should be noted that Dr. Chalmers, the great and dominant figure among those who then, for conscience' sake, left the Church of Scotland—or to speak more accurately left the State Establishment, taking with him a large section of the Church—was not in favour of disestablishment; that was not the issue on which the split came, true though it is that, as a result of developments subsequent to the disruption, establishment became, to some extent, a controversial issue in Scotland. Early in the present century the right of the United Free Church to the possession of its properties, which was challenged by a minority on the ground of departure from recognized doctrinal standards, came finally before the House of Lords in its judicial capacity, and judgment was given in 1904 in favour of those who came to be known as the Wee Frees. Despite the arguments of Mr. R. B. Haldane, afterwards Lord Haldane, who applied himself with all the zeal of a Hegelian philosopher to the subject of predestination and free-will, it was decided that such a doctrinal variation in the standards of orthodoxy had resulted from the union in 1900 of the Free Church and another body, the United Presbyterians, that the Free Church was not entitled to keep its properties, but that these must go to the dissentient minority. It was widely held that the situation could not be allowed to remain where the judgment had left it, and political action was taken in 1905 to preserve for the United Free Church majority the greater part of the resources of which the judgment had deprived it.

These events have, for the student of theology, the importance of revealing a claim to such an interpretation of documents as was consonant with the general mind of the Church at a time much later than that in which the documents were composed: to that extent they belong to the history of theology in Scotland. They do, moreover, show that the rigid doctrine of election and reprobation, which the Westminster Confession inherited from Calvin and shared with other confessions of faith of the sixteenth and seventeenth centuries, was increasingly felt to be at variance with the New Testament Gospel of the love of God manifested in the incarnation and cross of His Son. But they are not important as though they marked an actual turning-point in theology; their main interest is legal, and even political, rather than theological. One may take leave of them, and of Scottish ecclesiastical divisions with their relation to Church establishment, with the note that the reunion of the Church of Scotland and the United Free Church, fully accomplished in 1929, made of Scottish Presbyterianism an organized unity, with the exception of some minor bodies of no large size and tenaciously conservative in their beliefs and in their attitude to Biblical criticism.

This brings us to the second subject that occasioned acute division of opinion in Scotland during the last century. The consideration of the issues raised by the Higher Criticism came to the front in connexion with the teaching of Professor W. Robertson Smith, who held the chair of Hebrew and Old Testament criticism in the Free Church College of Aberdeen. The story has been told from different points of view by J. S. Black in *The Life of William Robertson Smith* and by Dr. Carnegie Simpson in *The Life of Principal Rainy*. No one who has read their pages can have failed to recognize the essential elements of tragic drama, a great and contentious theme, the enthusiasm for an inspiring teacher answered by the hardening of opposition to teaching that seemed destructive of a foundational truth, the sway of fortunes, the first triumph, the final overthrow of the man, if not of the cause for which he stood. Most dramatic of all is the picture of the gradual concentration of the controversy in all its aspects into one tremendous personal clash between two great protagonists, Robertson Smith and Robert Rainy, of whom the former, while he claimed that his tradition of scriptural interpretation was that of Luther and Calvin,

saw the whole controversy in terms of the right of the teacher
to proclaim the truth as he saw it; the latter, while not opposed
in principle to liberty of criticism, was deeply concerned for
such an outcome as would make for the well-being of the
Church and bring to an end a passionate and embittered debate.

Those years of conflict precede the *terminus a quo* of the
present work. Suffice it to say that the final act of the drama
took place when on the 24th of May, 1881, Robertson Smith,
on the motion of Rainy, was removed by the General Assembly
of the Free Church of Scotland from his professorial chair.
But the condemnation of the man did not carry with it the
condemnation of the " criticism " for which he stood, since
the libel, to use the technical Scottish phrase, which aimed at
the authoritative declaration of one particular doctrine of Holy
Scripture, had been dropped after events that had taken place
in the previous year. As to the part played by Principal Rainy
in the case it is likely that students thereof will always differ.
Of special interest is the opinion expressed by Dr. Carnegie
Simpson many years after he had written Rainy's Life, in a letter
to myself from which I quote:

" While I do not defend his every step in it, I am satisfied I am right in the
main contention, namely, that but for Rainy, the libel would have been carried to
its judicial conclusion, and *that* would have meant not only the removal of
Smith from his chair, but also a decision in principle against liberty of criticism
in the Free Church. The latter—after all, the essential thing—Rainy saved."

On two later occasions the General Assembly of the Free
Church had to take decisions in connexion with Biblical criticism.
In 1889 Dr. Marcus Dods was elected to fill the New Testament
chair of New College, Edinburgh. He was an eminent Biblical
scholar, but, in the eyes of that section of the Free Church
to which the title " the Highland host " was given, unsound on
the inspiration and inerrancy of Holy Scripture. At the same
time, Dr. A. B. Bruce of the Free Church College in Glasgow
was arousing adverse feeling by reason of statements that had
appeared in his published works. The teaching of the Professors
was examined by the College Committee and Sub-Committee
of the Assembly, which, while commenting more or less
severely on various statements in the works submitted to them,
came to the conclusion that " their writings do not afford
ground for instituting a process against either of them as teaching

what is at variance with the standards of the Church." On the basis of this the Assembly refused to initiate any process. It affirmed with unmistakable clearness the doctrines of our Lord's divinity, atonement, and resurrection, and deplored whatever might seem to disparage them as in any way dispensable. Further, the Assembly laid stress on the infallible truth and divine authority of the Holy Scriptures and appealed, in accordance with the Reformed tradition, to the inner testimony of the Holy Spirit. It pronounced the use of such terms as " mistakes " and " immoralities " in relation to recognized difficulties in the Scriptures as utterly unwarranted. All this had reference to Dr. Dods. Dr. Bruce was admonished for his manner of statement in respect of the inspiration of the Gospels, and of doctrinal matters, including our Lord's teaching. But no condemnation was passed, and it was regarded as permissible to hold a view of the Bible which did not claim for it verbal inerrancy. The Assembly would have been involved in far greater difficulties, and, indeed, might have been unable to refrain from such condemnation, had the libel in the Robertson Smith case which aimed at a doctrinal decision been carried to an affirmative conclusion. Of that case one may hear the final echo when in 1902 the Assembly refused to institute a process against Dr. G. A. Smith's book, *Modern Criticism and the Preaching of the Old Testament.*

Before we pass from this subject, the contribution which Scottish theologians have made to Biblical scholarship should be noted. Contemporary with Dods and Bruce (Bruce, it should be said, combined in a remarkable way Biblical interpretation and exposition with the work of the religious philosopher and apologist) was A. B. Davidson, perhaps the most alike to Driver of all the Scottish scholars. Sutherland Black in his *Life of William Robertson Smith* quotes from Davidson's commentary on Job to illustrate the fundamental position of what came to be known as " believing criticism." Davidson wrote: " The books of Scripture, so far as interpretation and general formal criticism are concerned, must be handled very much as other books are handled." The books are the Word of God, and we bow under their meaning when that is ascertained. But the intellectual treatment " must be mainly the same as we give to other books." To his name many would need to be added, were a full conspectus being made of the labours expended in the fields of Old Testament and New Testament study. A few may be taken as representative of a larger body. Dr. Denney was in the front rank of those scriptural interpreters for whom the first necessity was a precise exegesis of the text. Dr. G. A. Smith, besides his larger works, produced what is probably one of the most readable commentaries on an Old Testament book ever published, the two volumes on Isaiah in the Expositor's Bible. Dr. James Moffatt, who despite his long residence in America belongs to Scotland, has put numbers of readers of the Bible in his debt by his new translation, first of the New, then of the Old Testament. His *Introduction to the Literature of the New Testament* (1911) in the *International Theological Library* is still the most comprehensive survey of that field which exists in English. Dr. Adam Welch has paid special attention to questions concerning the religion of Israel and the date of Deuteronomy. Principal George Duncan of St. Andrews has been prominent in arousing fresh interest in the problem of the provenance of the " Captivity Epistles " of St. Paul. One of the most valuable books on the subject of eschatology in respect of its literary and historical background is Dr. J. H. Leckie's *The World to Come and Final Destiny* (1918).

On the other hand, it would be true to say that during the last twenty-five years less has been done in Scotland than in England for the interpretation of the New Testament, by close investigation of the theological background from which the writers started, and of the theology involved in what they said and what they implied. It is in their attention to this side of the New Testament, which for them is central, that the special value of the work of Sir Edwyn Hoskyns and Mr. Noel Davey consists. Detailed criticism of *The Riddle of the New Testament* (1931) and of *The Fourth Gospel* (1940) ought never to obscure the fact that in these works a method of study is pursued which, as a method, marks a new approach to the New Testament. The time of its appearance was the more opportune since it coincided with the increasing attention paid to the literary problems of the synoptic Gospels, involved in the attempt by means of Form-criticism (Formgeschichte) to penetrate more deeply into the materials used in the composition of the Gospels and the processes employed in the arrangement of the materials.

But if the study of Biblical theology has not been greatly

enriched of late from north of the Tweed, if, to refer to work that is on lines of research different from those pursued by Hoskyns and those who have come directly under his influence, there is nothing that can be ranked in importance with Streeter's *The Four Gospels* (1924), or with the thoroughgoing exposition of the New Testament foundations of the doctrine of the Atonement to which Dr. Vincent Taylor has devoted three successive books, that is far from implying that Scottish theology has become becalmed in a backwater. It is, as a survey of past and present will show, as attentive as ever to Christian doctrine and its relations with the philosophy of religion.

The history of theological thought and development in Scotland during the last sixty years is not separable from some account of the position adopted and the influence exerted by individual teachers. A clear-cut distinction between Scotland and England at this point cannot be made. Movements in England cannot be understood without attention given to the parts played, previous to and within the period covered by this book, by such theologians as Pusey, Maurice, and Gore among Anglicans, by Dale and Forsyth among Free Churchmen. They stamped a particular character upon tendencies that would have revealed themselves differently in their emphases, proportions, and even patterns had such personal forces been absent. Nevertheless, in England, the tendencies and movements have had a certain impersonal quality, because they have been related to a changing ecclesiastical situation, and, often, to controversial exigencies. With this the Scottish situation has had little in common. The scholars and theologians of Scotland have, with such exceptions as have been mentioned, been undisturbed by the " excursions and alarums " which their southern confrères have often been unable to ignore. They have influenced their age according to what has appeared to be the intrinsic value of their teaching; it has had little relation to current internal Church controversy: there has been little indeed of such controversy to which it could be related.

It seems to me, therefore, that the approach to any adequate (however inadequate) account of Scottish theology must be by way of particular theologians. It is necessary that the main features of the teaching of the relevant individuals should be described, with such comments upon developments or changes in the teaching as may help towards a more accurate historical picture.

Alexander Balmain Bruce, with whom we have already made contact in a brief account of the Dods-Bruce case, was for many years one of the most influential teachers in Scotland. In his book, *Persons and Ideals* (1939), Principal W. M. Macgregor says of him and A. B. Davidson that they " made a deeper mark for good upon the spirit of their men than any Scottish teacher since Chalmers." At the same time Dr. Macgregor notes his limitations: he " had little of the technical equipment of the scholar," nor anything of a " panoply of scientific learning "; and he took little interest in the traditional theology of his Church. Bruce was indeed curiously un- and even anti-ecclesiastical. In *The Miraculous Element in the Gospels* (1886) he asks the depressing question, " What is the whole history of the Church but a long, dreary winter of legalism with bright, calm, halcyon days of restored intuition intervening now and then?" Three years later he expressed himself still more strongly in the last chapter of *The Kingdom of God*, entitled " The Christianity of Christ." The ecclesiastical Christ was " to a large extent " not the Christ of the Gospels but a creation of scholastic theology, whereas " it is the Son of Man we need to know; not as denying His divinity but as knowing whom we affirm to be divine. . . . The vital matter is to confess that God is this well-known Man." The time called for one who, free " from ecclesiasticism, and dogmatism and sacramentarianism, . . . will have but one absorbing care and passion—to make the young know and love Jesus Christ." Critical of the imposition of existing creeds, Bruce wrote that " the task of an apologist is desperate if he is supposed to be the advocate of the *status quo* in theology. It is otherwise if he appears as the expositor or advocate of the Christianity of Christ."

It is not on the critical side of his mind that Bruce is particularly impressive. It is in his devotion to the Gospels and to the Person revealed in them that he stands out as a great religious teacher, as also in the moral fervour which forms a kind of luminous atmosphere for what he has to say. The note which he sounds in the comparatively early work that became so widely known, *The Training of the Twelve* (1871), echoes continually in his writings, though its tone is far less clear and appealing in

the article on Jesus Christ which at the end of his career he
contributed to the *Encyclopædia Biblica* (1901). To that article,
in so far as it suggests (it does no more than that—but perhaps
as much) a definite break with orthodox Christology, there
are a few passages in his books which point forwards. I have
referred to one which appears in *The Kingdom of God*. Yet that
is very far from being characteristic. Neither Bruce's heart
nor his mind was in sympathy with an estimate of the significance
of the historical Jesus that came short of a very definite affirmation of His divinity, by which Bruce meant what the Councils
of Nicæa and Chalcedon meant, though it is true that the conciliar
definition and the notion of conciliar authority had, as such,
little weight with him. Allowing for this, it is noteworthy how
little there is in Bruce in line with those " liberal " pictures of
Jesus which Schweitzer so critically describes. In *The Training
of the Twelve* he is at the furthest remove from them. In his
belief, both the omniscience of Jesus and, apparently, the inerrancy of the Gospels have a place. A Christianity " independent
of dogma " is pronounced to be impossible, and the discarding
of the creed would result in a fading into darkness of the Christianity to which it led.

In the works that intervene between this early book and the
Encyclopædia Biblica article Bruce certainly moved away from a
conservative attitude. The *Chief End of Revelation* (1881) shows
him as dissatisfied with what he regards as the traditional theory
both of miracle and of prophecy, though he abandons neither
the fact of miracle nor an element of prediction in prophecy.
He sees the hope of the future in a Church capable of distinguishing " between *doctrines* of faith and theological *dogmas*," and
the need of the Church as involving " certainty, concord and
a simplified creed." But that simplification is not equivalent
to a revision of Christology, as *The Miraculous Element in the
Gospels* (1886) makes very plain. There, after reviewing the
record given in the pages of the evangelists, he concludes that
the " One Miracle " is that of Christ's Person, the moral-
miracle of His holiness, and that such a miracle naturally has
" physical relations and aspects." In words which have in them
the whole substance of historic orthodoxy he declares that
Jesus, " the true eternal Son of God and the perfect Son of
Man," is the supreme miracle. With that orthodoxy there

is less complete harmony in his work, *The Kingdom of God* (1889),
to which I have already referred. The sharpness of Bruce's
criticism of " ecclesiasticism," and of the imposition of credal
orthodoxy, was not without effect upon the manner in which
he expressed his own belief, though change of terminology
does not necessarily involve change of the substance of doctrine.
Jesus as portrayed in the Gospels is, he writes, an " absolutely
true and full manifestation of the Divine Being." He and God
" are in spirit one "—a phrase, in itself, of doubtful interpretation. In commenting upon the text, found in the first and third
Gospels, where our Lord speaks of the mutual knowledge of
the Father and the Son, Bruce affirms that there are " no texts
in the synoptical Gospels in which Divine Sonship in the metaphysical sense is ascribed to Jesus in a perfectly clear, indisputable
manner," though there are passages which hint at it.

The assertion of the ethical consciousness of Jesus Godwards
has close affinity with the teaching of Ritschl. A growing dislike
of metaphysics in theology is revealed in what he says of the
Baptismal formula. Its authenticity is not necessarily to be
denied: Bruce, again like Ritschl, was not a radical critic.
Jesus taught His disciples to regard God as their Father and
Himself as God's Son, " the revealer of the Father and the
prototype of Sonship," and was not silent concerning the
Spirit. But such teaching does not make it necessary to
identify " the rudimentary, moral and religious Trinity of the
Gospel with the developed, metaphysical, and speculative
Trinity of theology." Bruce's interpretation of the Kingdom
was on ethical, not eschatological lines. The parable of the seed
growing secretly (St. Mark iv. 26 ff.) is the clearest statement
in the New Testament of laws of growth obtaining in the
Kingdom; that Christ taught an early *parousia* is incompatible
with His declaration of the Son's ignorance of the day.

Tendencies and interests already noted reappear in *Apologetics*
(1892) and *St. Paul's Conception of Christianity* (1894). In the former
book he speaks again in accents familiar to the student of
Ritschl, and very different from anything that we could read
to-day in the pages of Dr. Karl Barth—except for the opening
words. Thus he writes: " All we really know of God in spirit
and in very truth we know through Jesus; but only on condition
that we truly know Jesus Himself as revealed to us in the pages

of the evangelic history. Knowledge of the historical Jesus is the foundation at once of a sound Christian theology and of a thoroughly healthy Christian life." Precise Ritschlian terminology appears when he speaks of Jesus as having for the Christian consciousness, and for the Apostolic Church, " the religious value of God." The tensions, unmistakably present in Bruce's attitude to formulated doctrine, are illustrated in his comments upon the significance of this value-judgment. As to metaphysical presuppositions of Christ's divinity opinions will differ. Aversion from conciliar definitions does not mean a denial of Christ's divinity, and may be a passing phase of aversion to precise theological terminology, and yet compatible with an attitude of heart towards Jesus fully sympathetic with the faith of the Catholic Church, " even in the most orthodox generations." As to revelation itself, Bruce regards its function as consisting not in the impartation of truths which the human mind cannot conceive, but in the conversion of conceivable possibilities into indubitable realities, for instance, the fancy of God as a Father into a sober fact. As in his earlier work devoted to the subject, he expounds miracle and prophecy as integral parts of revelation, not as evidential adjuncts to revelation.

The work on St. Paul is notable for its discussions of the Apostle's doctrines of sin and atonement and justification. Here, as always, Bruce goes his own way. He is profoundly concerned to show the ethical implications of the Pauline theology, while, at the same time, his accuracy and insight as an expositor of St. Paul's language save him from such an error of interpretation as that which deduces God's act of justification from His intention to sanctify. And as an interpreter of the " Grace " at the end of 2 Corinthians, he hardly avoids, certainly for the Apostle, by implication for himself, an advance well within the borders of metaphysics. The text suggests the Godhead of the Lord Jesus, since He is " named together with God and the energy of God as a source of blessing," and the " Three august Beings " are to be regarded as " bound together by the tie of a common divine nature."

In 1897 and 1898 Bruce was Gifford Lecturer and took as his subject, first *The Providential Order of the World*, next *The Moral Order of the World*. He showed himself ready to accept the evolutionary theory of man's origin without reservation;

the phenomena of mind, he says in the former work, need not imply a " distinct substratum," but in course of evolution may have arisen " in some quite inscrutable way out of what is called matter." The doctrine of the Incarnation he now brought into closest connexion with a belief, not as common then as it has since become, in divine passibility. The doctrine that Christ is God Incarnate " makes God a moral hero, a burden-bearer for His own children, a sharer in the sorrow and pain that come on the good through the moral evil that is in the world. The noble army of martyrs have the comfort of knowing that the Eternal Spirit is at their head. Christ is the visible human embodiment of His leadership." In the second course Bruce develops the conception of the relation existing between God and man, to which he had already given expression in *The Kingdom of God*. Jesus, he declares, taught specifically " that man as such stands indefeasibly in the relation of a son to God. All men indiscriminately are God's sons," the difference being that some do and others do not show themselves worthy of the title. Later he describes as " the very light of life " the belief " that the human and the divine are essentially one in the moral sphere." His sympathy with what he calls the Ethical Movement is combined with an insistence that it must become " an Ethical Theism," and with the hope that what lies ahead is " a better acquaintance with and a growing appreciation of the Galilæan Gospel."

The article on Jesus in the *Encyclopædia Biblica* published shortly after Bruce's death (he died in 1899) is less of a summing up of his prolonged studies of the Gospels than might have been expected. It came as a surprise, even as a shock, to those who had thought of Bruce's liberalism in theology as stopping well short of any break with the historic faith in respect of the Person of Christ. It would, indeed, be untrue to say that the article involves such a break; it is rather a case of the final question asked but not answered, and of a concentration upon what is actually given and made plain in the historical records, without an attempt to construe their doctrinal consequences. Thus, early in the article Bruce writes: " We see in Mark . . . the real man Jesus, without the aureole of faith around his head, yet with a glory of truth, wisdom, and goodness the better seen on that very account." Later, after a careful discussion of miracle, which shows him, as in previous works, inclining to accept the truth of the narratives, he concludes that for theology the question is whether we are brought face to face with a *man* fully endowed with powers dormant in ordinary men, or whether we have passed into " the region of the strictly divine." Our Lord's Messianic consciousness he interprets as inclusive of the Isaianic ideal of the suffering servant, and goes on to say that Jesus " thought of himself as . . . the representative of all who live sacrificial and therefore redemptive lives." How far this is consonant with the apostolic faith in Christ as the one Redeemer is not clear.

Of Christ as the supreme Teacher he writes plainly enough: " His spiritual intuitions are pure truth valid for all ages. God, man, and the moral ideal cannot be more truly or happily conceived ": we are only beginning to perceive the significance of His thought on these themes and of His " radical doctrine of the dignity of man." But one may well ask whether one who expresses this kind of appreciation of the teaching of Christ is not closer in sympathy to Harnack, whose lectures on *What is Christianity?* were nearly contemporaneous with Bruce's article, than to Gore, whose Bampton Lectures on *The Incarnation of the Son of God* preceded it by a few years. It is, I think, not unfair to say that Bruce's pages are curiously colourless, and give an impression of detachment, as though the writer were anxious not to commit himself too far. The atmosphere is quite different from that of William Sanday's corresponding article in Hastings' *Dictionary of the Bible*. It would be an improper conclusion that Bruce had abandoned Catholic Christology for that of Socinus; but his increasingly critical attitude towards the credal and ecclesiastical sides of Christianity, combined with a very strong grasp of the reality and significance of the perfection of humanity revealed in Christ, affected the direction of his thought and his intellectual sympathies.

Bruce, as Gifford Lecturer, had occasion to deal with problems that arise in the sphere of what it has been customary to call natural as distinct from revealed religion. But it was the moral not the metaphysical side of philosophy that attracted him. Of arguments that aimed at the construction of a fabric of rational theology he was not appreciative. Very different in this was his contemporary Robert Flint, Professor of Divinity in the University of Edinburgh. Flint was one of the most eminent philosophical theologians of his day; his work reveals a powerful mind, endowed with a logical ability and a robust commonsense that made him no less formidable as a critic than impressive as a constructive expositor of theistic and Christian belief. His three chief books bear the titles *Theism* (1877), *Anti-Theistic Theories* (1879), and *Agnosticism* (1903). Characteristic of the whole bent of his thought are the words that stand near the beginning of *Theism*, that the self-surrender of the soul " cannot be independent of reason and yet reasonable." Again and again he insists on the function of reason in relation to religious knowledge. In *Theism* he insists that we have no right to believe more than we know, and goes on to say that " if I have no reason for believing that there is a God, I have no right to believe that there is a God. . . . Belief is inseparable from knowledge and ought to be precisely co-extensive with knowledge," which may appear a hard saying, not easily reconcilable with St. Paul's declaration that " we know in part." In his assertion of the claims of human reason Flint stood much more in the tradition which, in the early Church, we associate with the theologians of Alexandria, and in later times with the Schoolmen, and particularly with St. Thomas Aquinas, than with the sixteenth-century Reformers, especially Luther. A wide gulf separates him from Karl Barth, whose Gifford Lectures are written from a very different standpoint.

Thus, in *Theism*, he maintains that a certain amount of knowledge of God may be reached through data furnished by perception and consciousness. Natural religion he describes as the foundation of all theology, just as the law of nature is the foundation of all ethical and political science. He asks, with reference to what may be found in the works of Plato, Cicero, and Seneca, whether there is " any heathen religion or heathen philosophy in which there are not truths of natural religion." Modern controversy on this subject gives a special relevance, whatever be thought of Flint's own attitude, to his verdict on the consequence of reliance upon a faith which implies our " intellectual disability with reference to divine things," instead of a search for manifestations of God's moral character in His works: that means, he declares, that we " should abandon ourselves to blind and irrational belief, and then proclaim that this foolish procedure is the true vindication of the ways of God to men." And in criticism of Luther and of a number of the Reformers he protests that they " ascribed to Scripture a position inconsistent with an adequate recognition either of the rights of reason or of the divine instructiveness of creation, providence, and man's own body and spirit."

The tone does not change in the much later work *Agnosticism* (1903). There too he insists on the duty of a sufficient reason for belief, which rests upon definite evidence, while, at the same time, he does not conceive of belief as an act with which the intellect alone is concerned. But Flint was convinced that any attempt to divorce religion from coherent thinking was a disastrous error. He would have nothing to do with the kind of religious agnosticism involved in the position of Sir William Hamilton and Dean Mansel, who denied to the human intellect the capacity for positive knowledge of God. Arguing against Dr. Paul Carus he insisted on the necessity for ideas of eternity and infinity in connexion with man's thought, and that apart from them there was " little room for rational faith in God or enlightened piety towards God." What he regarded as loose terminology was abhorrent to him. About the time when this book appeared, Ernst Haeckel's *Riddle of the Universe* was attracting much attention. Haeckel found a place for a religious attitude, even for religious belief, by his identification of God with the ether. On which Flint comments that " the word God has a definite meaning, and no man has any more right to identify it with the Ether than with a stock or a stone." One may be fully sympathetic with the tenor and intention of this protest, and yet remember that the word " God," in different languages and traditions, has been patient of a number of meanings, even though in all of them a sense of transcendent reality, however crudely and unphilosophically expressed, is to be recognized.

Ritschl would have expelled metaphysics from theology: he was also severely critical of mysticism. Flint held that in theology metaphysics were a necessary, and mysticism a very valuable, element. He deals with mysticism in the volume *On Theological, Biblical and Other Subjects* (1905); and his judgment is that " whatever be its faults and shortcomings it has often been of great service, and carries with it a large fund of truth, which the theologian of no period can afford to despise or neglect. . . . No worthy theologian will deny profound obligations to the great masters of mystic theology. No hours can be spent by the theologian better than with some of the mystics." As an appreciation of mysticism, this does not fall far short of what Dr. Inge would have, and has, written; as a criticism of the Ritschlian attitude, which W. Herrmann, of whom I would always speak with profound respect, represented, it might be said *plus royaliste que le roi*, Flint's words are, by implication, no less severe than those that Dr. Inge used in *Personal Idealism and Mysticism* (1907). One particular statement of Harnack, the most learned of all those who may be described as of the school of Ritschl, met with specially sharp censure from Dr. Inge. It is worth recalling in view of Flint's observations on the subject. Harnack said that mysticism was typical Catholic piety. Flint regarded mysticism as overpassing ecclesiastical boundaries. There were both Protestant and Catholic mystics; the latter, however, had been willing to make their doctrines " subservient to the interests of their Church." He continues: " I am inclined to think that there has been too much mysticism in the Catholic and too little in the Protestant Church."

Flint did not lose the scriptural theologian in the philosopher of religion. That is clearly shown in the book last mentioned. There he describes apologetics as an instrument and dogmatics as an end, and it is from Scripture that he derives and expounds the truth which is formulated in dogmatics. The central principle of Scripture, he declares, in language reminiscent of Bishop Butler, to be " the mediatorial principle which reached ultimate realization in an atoning death." This central principle reappears in Christian theology, all parts of which " equally refer " to " Christ as Mediator." Only by " participation in the righteousness, love, and grace revealed in Him " is the human race raised from " the eternal death in which it by nature lies." That is the scriptural teaching concerning the purpose of Christ's coming. This is the historic language of the Reformed tradition in Christian theology, and in that tradition Flint stood, whatever criticisms he might make of the Reformers' depreciation of the value of human reason in respect of the knowledge of God. His reliance upon Scripture did not involve what we now know as " fundamentalism." Free research into the character and credibility of the Biblical books he regarded as not " unwarranted and profane." In some " findings " of those who investigated such problems he discerned the presence of metaphysical assumptions—for instance, as to the impossibility of miracle.

The value of the teaching that Flint gave of the rational character of that theistic belief which Christian theology assumes, and of the capacity of the human mind for a knowledge which does not stop short of a real knowledge of God, was the greater because of the atmosphere of doubtfulness which seemed to many to result from the Darwinian theory. It was not infrequently supposed that Darwin had undermined the theistic case. Flint knew that no such claim was made by Darwin himself. Writing in *Agnosticism* he says of the great scientist: "No man, placed as he was, could have given less encouragement to the folly of those who would fain have raised him to the rank of an authority in theology." It is in keeping with Flint's appeal to reason for the vindication and protection of faith that he maintains that righteousness and love in God cannot mean " something wholly different in kind from what is meant by them in man." John Stuart Mill had said very much the same thing. A theism which should deny this would be quite different from what is more than implicit in the Biblical revelation.

With all his interest in philosophy and his innate capacity for metaphysical discussion, Flint gave his adherence to no one school of philosophical interpretation. We pass into a very different atmosphere as we come to the consideration of the two eminent teachers closely associated with the University of Glasgow, John and Edward Caird, the one ending his career (in 1898) as Principal thereof, and the other being for a number of years (1866-93) Professor of Moral Philosophy, before he became Master of Balliol in succession to Jowett. There can be no doubt as to the tradition which they followed and the conception of reality which they expounded. It is that which has as its most famous representative Hegel. But just because there has been no agreed interpretation of Hegel's doctrine, particularly in relation to Christian theology, the adjective " Hegelian " as attached to a philosopher or theologian is not self-explanatory. With regard to John Caird, that is made plain in the memoir which his brother wrote in 1899 as an introduction to the Principal's Gifford Lectures on *The Fundamental Ideas of Christianity*. He says of him that " the conviction that God can be known and is known, and that in the deepest sense all our knowledge

is knowledge of Him, was the corner-stone of his theology."
He goes on to remark that his brother was entirely at one with
Hegel in his trust in the powers of the human intelligence, and
in refusing to seek safety for religion in feeling, in the moral
consciousness, " or in some form of æsthetic or religious
intuition, which is to be regarded as above reason and exempt
from criticism." On the other hand, " if Hegelianism is, as
some tell us, the resolution of the life of the world into some
spectral woof of impalpable abstractions, or unearthly ballet
of bloodless categories; if it is the substitution of the theory of
reality for reality itself; if it is a system that resolves man into
a mere *modus* of the divine, or God into the poetic substantiation
of an abstraction—and all these things have been said of Hegel;
if it even means a denial of the substantial truth of the ordinary
Christian consciousness, and the substitution for it of a philosophical theory, then my brother was not a Hegelian." Edward
Caird points to *An Introduction to the Philosophy of Religion* (1880)
and to the attack upon such notions contained in that volume.
But neither John nor Edward could allow of any sharp contrast
between philosophy and theology, between faith and reason.
The essential harmony which John Caird found to exist is
expressed in this summation: " Christianity and Idealism were
the two poles of my brother's thinking, and the latter seemed to
him the necessary means for interpreting the former." One can,
indeed, hardly imagine a feeling more at odds with the attitude
to the capacities of the human reason, in respect of religious
truth, which the name of Karl Barth suggests, than the repugnance
of John Caird to any theories which " empty reason of its
religious content."

The Cairds were at one in their general outlook; nevertheless, a difference between them is to be noted, and there are
words of Edward which show that he was conscious of it. It
would not be true to say that, where the distinctive Christian
doctrines of the Incarnation and the Trinity were concerned,
John kept his idealistic philosophy in the background. But he did
not regard it as a principle of thought that necessitated a definite
and considerable reinterpretation of Christian doctrine. John
was not primarily a metaphysician as his brother was. He was a
minister of the Church of Scotland, and he had been in charge of a
parish before the call came to him to be Professor of Divinity

in the University. The theological tradition, as understood and operative in a Christian society, was near to his heart. One might perhaps say that whereas Edward lays stress upon Christianity as the religious climax, John, without wishing to deny that, is conscious also of an element of contrast, of that within Christianity which distinguishes it from other religions. Thus, while in the Gifford Lectures he argues against an antithesis of natural and revealed religion, he affirms that "there is not a single doctrine of natural religion which, when it enters into the content of the Christian faith, remains what it was outside of Christianity." He is as convinced as Edward Caird shows himself to be in his own first series of Gifford Lectures, *The Evolution of Religion* (1893), that the cardinal Christian doctrine is that of "the unity of God and man," and as much prepared to emphasize "the self-revelation of God in humanity." But in his doctrine of God there is more definite weight attached to those articles of the Christian creed in which Christian theology passes beyond the findings of any philosophy of religion.

Thus, when he writes of the ascription to God of an intellectual and moral nature, he sees no possibility of arriving at such a point except "by that conception which is expressed in the Christian doctrine of the Logos or Son of God—the conception of a self-revealing principle or personality within the very essence of the Godhead." This is wholly in accord with an earlier statement that "the Trinity is the distinctively Christian idea of God," and with what he goes on to say in a later passage with regard to the Person of Christ, that "there is something unique in the Person of Christ, and that a participation in the being and life of God can be predicated of Him as distinguished from all other members of the human race." This "something" he later defines as "a principle . . . which had its source and origin in the eternal being and life of God," and describes the ideal divine-human life as realized in Christ as "a human consciousness possessed and suffused by the very spirit and life of the living God." In view of this theology, which derives from the New Testament passages in which the pre-existence of the Logos or Son is declared, and is in line with the historic formulations of the doctrine of the Incarnation, it is curious that when he comes to a discussion of the Kenotic theory, of which he is critical, he quite ignores the bearing of the notion of pre-existence and its implications. And I think that in his work as a whole there is more than a suggestion of a tension between his metaphysical idealism and his theology, and that his interpretation of the latter by the former presented more difficulties than Edward Caird allowed for in the words that I have quoted from the memoir.

Two further points in Principal Caird's exposition of Christian " ideas " may be noted. In connexion with the Atonement he is reminiscent of McLeod Campbell and anticipatory of Moberly. " Conceive," he says, ". . . the ideal of moral perfection incarnate in a human personality, and at the same time one who loves us with a love so absolute as to identify himself with us, and to make our good and evil his own—bring together these elements in a living, conscious, human spirit, and you have in it a capacity of shame and sorrow and anguish, a possibility of bearing the burden of human guilt and wretchedness, which lost and human humanity can never bear for itself." It is interesting to note that in the memoir his strong approval of the conferring of the degree of D.D. upon McLeod Campbell by the University of Glasgow is recorded. Then, on the relation of God to the sorrow of the world, Principal Caird was critical of the doctrine of divine impassibility. He and Dr. A. M. Fairbairn, the eminent Principal of Mansfield College, Oxford, were, perhaps, the two most notable predecessors of those theologians and religious teachers who have held and expounded the belief that God is a " suffering God." I was unaware of this when I wrote my book *The Impassibility of God.*

John Caird's gifts as a religious thinker, deeply concerned to appeal to his hearers, not least to the student class, receive very full illustration in the *University Sermons* published in 1898. As a parish minister he had made a great impression by his eloquence, and that eloquence was not lost, though, doubtless, held more in check, when he preached in the University Chapel. In his sermons he is more Biblical and less metaphysical, and his devotion to the Person of Christ is manifest. The essence of religion he declares to be found in " love and loyalty to Christ as the one only Redeemer and Lord of the spirit." He strongly emphasizes the witness to Christ " in the living experience of every Christian heart." Preaching on " Heredity in the Spiritual Life " he says: " This, at least, we know, that, be heaven what or where it may, they will never find themselves unprepared for it who, filled with undying faith in Christ's promise, have in life and death identified their own happiness with the cause for which He lived and died, the final triumph of the Kingdom of light and love, the Kingdom of Christ in the world." His essentially tolerant and generous spirit is revealed in a moving passage in which he speaks of John Henry Newman's *Apologia* and of Francis Newman's *Phases of Faith*. But Caird was no light-hearted optimist, shutting his eyes to the darker possibilities of human life and the sterner aspects of Christian truth. He can speak of " a sinful soul . . . in its guilty anguish, as of a worm that dieth not and a fire that is not quenched," and of " the easy, good-natured divinity who makes everything comfortable " as " not the God of the Bible."

Principal Caird was not, and did not aspire to be, a great Church leader. From the institutional side of religion he obviously stood aloof: he was not a master of religious assemblies. But the memoir makes plain, with the testimonies that are incorporated in it, how real was his influence and how much he counted in that academical life, which needs, but does not always know that it needs, the inspiration and guidance of the Spirit of Christ.

If in John Caird the theologian and the philosopher were not quite at one, that certainly could not be said of his younger brother. Edward Caird was one of the most distinguished philosophers of his time, and of the honour in which he was held there could be no more sufficient proof than that he was elected to succeed Benjamin Jowett as Master of Balliol. His three chief published works are *The Critical Philosophy of Immanuel Kant* (1889) and the two series of Gifford Lectures. Convinced of the adequate and comprehensive character of the idealistic philosophy, he had no hesitation, not only as to the possibility, but as to the rightness, if not the necessity, of an alliance between it and religion, particularly religion in its highest form, that is in Christianity. He was too strong and independent a thinker to give his allegiance to any one philosophical master, however eminent; but it would not be unfair to describe Edward Caird as a Hegelian who saw in the conceptions of Hegel concerning God and the world, concerning reconciliation and unity, the most fruitful of truths both for philosophy and for theology. In the history of man's religion he saw a process of development from lower to higher forms, and his first series of Gifford Lectures, *The Evolution of Religion* (1893), is of the nature of a commentary upon that process. On this development as justifying religious faith he speaks with a confidence that would be much more rarely found to-day. He thinks of God as "a spiritual principle manifested in all nature and history," and declares that " it would be acknowledged by almost everyone that we are now shut up to the alternative *either* that there is no God and no revelation or knowledge of Him, *or* that the revelation of God must be sought in the whole process of nature and history, regarded as a development which finds its ultimate end and its culminating expression in the life of man as a spiritual being."

Caird's trust in the power of human reason for the attainment of truth, with which went a strong aversion from the *via negativa* of mysticism, as though truth could be reached through the method of abstraction, derived naturally from his conception of the relation between God the infinite Mind and finite centres of consciousness. The movement of modern thought in various forms converged on the conclusion that "we cannot think of the infinite Being as a will which is external to that which it has made; we cannot, indeed, think of Him as external to anything, least of all to the spiritual beings who, as such, live, move and have their being in Him." Both in *The Evolution of Religion* and in the later Gifford Lectures on *The Evolution of Theology in the Greek Philosophers* (1904) we meet with the notion of the idea of God pointing the way to the overcoming of the contrast between the self and the not-self, between subject and object. A sentence in the second series puts this very clearly—where Caird affirms that " God is a word that has no significance, unless by it we mean to express the idea of a Being who is the principle of unity presupposed in all the differences of things, and in all our divided consciousness of them."

Any consideration of Caird's attitude to Christianity, both as religion and as theology, should start with a full recognition of his conviction that his emphasis upon unity was entirely in line with the teaching of Christ and with the implications of the doctrine of His Person. Caird would never have allowed that in his conception of the unity of the human spirit with the divine he was transforming Christianity according to a metaphysical pattern. On the contrary, in the consciousness of Christ he

saw that unity realized: " Jesus Christ, we may say, first dis-
covered man's true relation to God and lived in it. . . . So long
as the conscience of man retains its power, it must acknowledge,
though it may be with greatly changed forms of doctrinal
interpretation, that the divine and human were brought together
in one whose consciousness of unity with God so directly
passed into a consciousness of unity with man." Man's sonship
to God " Jesus, as the Messiah, claims for Himself that He may
claim it for men." Caird finds this meaning involved in the
title " Son of Man." It was not in the confession of this unity
between the divine and human as real in Jesus, but in the
restriction of it to Him that Caird holds that Christian theology
was astray, as early as the teaching of St. Paul, who introduced
" a kind of separation of Christ from humanity and a kind of
identification of him with God, which is practically a return to
the Jewish opposition of God and man, and a denial of the
distinctive title which Christ gave to himself as the Son of Man."
The whole notion of the *deus absconditus* and of the *scandalon*
involved in the appearance of Jesus on the stage of history, with
which the Biblical theology of Hoskyns and his followers, and
the dogmatic of the Barthians, has made our age familiar, is
altogether alien from anything that Caird would have thought.

The metaphysical identification of the real with the rational,
which one specially connects with the philosophy of Hegel, is
to be discerned in Caird's conception of Christology. One
of the letters which are printed in the attractive and informing
biography by Sir Henry Jones and Professor Muirhead contains
a passage that is illuminating when it is regarded in contrast with
the Catholic doctrine of Christ's Godhead. " I cannot but
think," writes Caird, " that Christ becomes much greater in
reality when we recognize Him as a great moral genius (if one
might use the word), working His way to a higher conception
of spiritual reality, with the common limitations of men in
relation to the future expression of His own thought. We can
get so far as to have the glimpse of a gradual, though never
quite complete, conquest over the apocalyptic view—of a
Messiah bringing in a catastrophic judgment of the world—by
the idea of spiritual development." It is noteworthy that
hardly any title ascribed to Christ is viewed with more thorough-
going aversion by the modern theologians to whom I have

referred than that of " genius." And I think it must be said that
Caird read into the Gospels an accord with what he, as a philosopher, held to be true, which scholars of different schools
would not accredit.

At the same time, it would be quite unfair to give the impression that Caird minimized the divergence of his teaching from
that of historic orthodoxy. A very definite challenge is involved
in his assertion that the belief in the revelation of a divine
spirit in man and nature was the one " article of a standing or a
falling Church," and that " it is the rock upon which the
Christian Church is really founded, and from which it could be
built up if every ecclesiastical organization that exists were
destroyed." His dislike of the idea of " an irruption of the
spiritual into the natural world " comes out in his attitude towards the Resurrection of Christ. That there were visions of
the risen Christ he does not dispute, though he gives no opinion
as to their nature, such as Keim did when he propounded the
well-known suggestion of a " telegram from heaven." But he
will not admit anything that involves what we should call
miracle, for which he affirms that there is no real evidence.
The notion of " irruption " he regarded as inconsistent with
the idea that the natural world " is spiritual in its own right—as
the common doctrine of the divinity of Christ can only be very
artificially reconciled with the idea of the revelation of God in
man." His whole standpoint may be summed up in a sentence
that he wrote in a letter of the year 1891: " I feel that the time
has come for the old bottles to be broken, and that it is the new
wine of Christianity itself that must break them, if Christianity
and humanity are ever to be one."

Whether Caird's theology was au fond pantheistic is a question
on which agreement is unlikely. An American student of his
writings, W. Preston Warren, author of *Pantheism in Neo-
Hegelian Thought* (1933), gives reasons for an affirmative answer,
relying, for instance, on such words of Caird's as those in which
he speaks of " the ultimate presupposition of our consciousness "
being an " absolute unity," which transcends even the " opposition of subject and object." He interprets Caird's system as
one in which " there is but one genuine reality, and that reality
is God," as a " monism in which the finite consciousness must
lose all distinct reality," though he allows that there are what

he calls " concrete trends " which find a place for the " reality of concrete existence." On the other hand, a simple identification of God with the universe is not consistent with Caird's notions of immanence and manifestation. Reference may be made to two passages in the later Gifford Lectures on *The Evolution of Theology in the Greek Philosophers*. In one, where he is recalling his evaluation of the religious consciousness in the earlier lectures, he describes its essential meaning as " the consciousness of a Being who embraces all our life and gives unity and direction to it, who lifts us above ourselves, and binds our limited and transitory existence to the eternal." In the other he comes to the consideration of the problem which the attentive student of Plato knows well, whether the idea of the good is equivalent to the idea of God. His answer is that " the unity of being and knowing, if we take it positively, cannot be conceived except as an absolute self-consciousness, a creative mind, whose only object is a universe which is the manifestation of itself." Not only such passages as these, but the impression which Caird's manner of speaking of God conveys, make it hard to conclude that for Caird the unity of the human and the divine, of the universe and God, rules out anything of a real distinction.

Certainly Caird is not open to the charge that the universe, as he conceives it, is a " static " or " block " universe in which nothing happens and the whole notion of progress is inadmissible. Stoic pantheism did involve that doctrine by its ideas of determinism and of recurrent circular motion, and it was against modern idealistic variants of that doctrine, as he interpreted them, that William James protested. But for Caird the notion of development was of the first importance in his philosophy. What he says of evil is in point here: he did not deny " the reality of sin and misery "; to this element in the world " full justice " must be done: " but," he continues, " the positive overreaches it and transforms it unto good."

As in the case of his brother, the idea of " a Suffering God " is to be found. This, however, is not directly affirmed in the Gifford Lectures; but his biographers draw attention to a paper he read at a society, in early Oxford days before the Glasgow professorship, in which he insisted on the truth of " a God not only manifesting Himself, but participating and ' involved ' in the movement of man's history." With many later exponents of this conception, it has been most closely linked with Christ's suffering and death. Whether any stress was laid on this in the paper in question I do not know; but it must be said that the particular concentration upon the Cross, which is the great evangelical note in Christianity and transcends differences of Church order and communion, is not present in Caird's work. The dependence upon Christ, who, as St. Paul puts it, " loved me and gave himself for me," is something very different from the recognition of Christ as " the man in whom the universal spirit of humanity has found its fullest expression," as " the ideal or typical man, the Son of Man . . . who reveals what is in humanity, *just because* He is the purest revelation of God in man." No one, I think, could read the works of Edward Caird, including the *Lay Sermons* (1907) which he delivered from time to time in Balliol, and be surprised at the influence which he exercised. Few philosophers can have been more intent on seeing the phenomena of all existence *sub specie æternitatis*, and few can have given a deeper impression of grave nobility of character. But if neo-Hegelianism has failed, as they say, " to stay the course," that may be due more than a little to the ultimate impossibility of uniting its vision of God and the universe with that which is given in the New Testament.

No theologian of his time ranged over a wider field than Dr. James Orr, who held a Professorial Chair in the Free Church College in Glasgow. Church History and Dogmatics were probably the subjects in which he was most at home from the standpoint of strict scholarship; but his work reveals also a very competent Biblical theologian and one well acquainted with the philosophy of religion. He wrote what has been regarded as the most powerful attack upon the main theories associated with the Higher Criticism of the Old Testament in his book *The Problem of the Old Testament* (1906). He published two studies of Ritschlianism, *The Ritschlian Theology and the Evangelical Faith* (1897), and *Ritschlianism: Expository and Critical Essays* (1903), and was undoubtedly a very able critic, never unfair if rarely sympathetic. In his latter years he seems to have become increasingly conservative, notably in respect of the doctrine of man, an attitude that carried with it hostility to the Darwinian theory of evolution.

His arguments show great care in preparation and abundant

attention to detail. I find it hard not to think that at times he tries to prove too much; thus, in *The Resurrection of Jesus* (1908), which is, in general, an impressive defence of the historic Christian faith that "on the third day He rose again from the dead," his attempt to construct a single unified picture of the events of the first Easter day is hardly likely to satisfy at every point a reader who does not feel obliged to postulate complete accuracy in the evangelists' narratives. On this question Orr came very near to a doctrine of Biblical inerrancy. It is true that in *Revelation and Inspiration* (1910) he will not defend the view that "the *ipsissima verba* of the original autographs" are free from the slightest taint of error, but his sympathies and emphases point clearly in the direction of a position that is not far removed from it. Laying stress on the fact that the Bible has constantly been found to be correct in what it says, he continues: "On this broad general ground the advocates of 'inerrancy' may always feel that they have a *strong position*, whatever assaults may be made on them in matters of lesser detail." On the other hand he repudiates "mechanical" inspiration, and remarks that such a theory may be held "to imply a *literality* in narratives, quotations or reports of discourses, which the facts as we know them do not warrant." Instancing reports of our Lord's sayings, he concludes that "the end is gained if the *meaning* of the saying is preserved, though the precise form of words varies." This the advocates of verbal inspiration are, he affirms, compelled to recognize. Whatever be thought of Orr's standpoint, he does make it quite clear that the conception of verbal inspiration is not as simple as some would suppose, and that inerrancy cannot be pressed so far as to involve a record precisely coincident with the original.

Orr's tenacious conservatism, when he is concerned with the Bible, is not inconsistent with, but does not prepare us for, the width of outlook which he displays as a systematic theologian, when he is writing positively, and not controversially and in criticism of others. *The Progress of Dogma* (1901) has its critical side, for Orr has constantly in mind the account which Harnack gives of the developments of Christian thought in the most important of all his works, *The History of Dogma*. Nevertheless, Orr's much shorter work is not overcharged with comment upon Harnack's judgments; positively it is an admirably lucid narrative of doctrinal issues, movements and settlements. Strong Protestant as he was, Orr could not approach the controversies of the sixteenth century without bias; but bias here stands for the reality of personal belief, for a decision of acceptance and of refusal, from which no Christian historian of events and ideas, which have divided and do divide Christians, can claim to be exempt. With this reservation, Orr may certainly be given the title of an objective, not a partisan, writer. He was, one may suggest, conscious of having a great theme which deserved to be expounded with a due appreciation of all that had been gained in the past, and of the progress that might be made in the future towards fuller knowledge of the truth. Orr had a far greater understanding of the value of the dogmatic theology, which the Church of the present had inherited from the Church of the early centuries, than Bruce possibly ever achieved, certainly than Bruce would have recognized as of importance for the theologian of to-day. And while it would be a false judgment if one were to say that Harnack's great work embodies a radically pessimistic outlook, there is unquestionably a pessimistic side to it, which reveals itself especially in connexion with the early period, when the lines of advance were being consciously or unconsciously laid, and with the doctrinal crises when they reached their goal. From Orr's pages any such pessimism is quite absent.

Dr. Orr's most impressive work is his volume of Kerr Lectures, published under the title *The Christian View of God and the World* (1893). It is a most able and well-balanced contribution to doctrinal theology; it is earlier than any of his books already mentioned, but shows no sign of immaturity. It has its controversial side, but is, as a whole, expository and constructive. Like Flint he affirms a real knowledge of God which man can reach by the exercise of his rational powers, and neither in these Lectures, nor in his later criticisms of Ritschl and his school, does he hesitate to give a place to metaphysics and to mysticism in theology. Thus he writes: "If God is, thought must be able, nay is compelled, to take account of His existence." Theism is the rational conclusion of human enquiry into the phenomena of nature, but it "needs revelation to complete it." He asserts the fact of man's sonship—"as made by God, and as standing in his normal relation to Him, man is without doubt a son "—and he speaks approvingly of the idea of "an essential kinship which

exists between the human spirit and the Divine.'' In the later
of his two volumes against the Ritschlians he writes emphatically:
'' To say that in the revelation of Christ *only* we have knowledge
of God, that there is no such thing as natural theology or any
rational evidence for the existence of God, is practically to make
the understanding an atheist ''; and consonantly with this, in
God's Image in Man he denies that sin has resulted in the complete
effacement in man of that image.

His teaching on this subject prepares the way for his exposition
of the doctrine of the Incarnation. Holding that there is a
'' bond between God and man '' which is '' inner and essential,''
and, more particularly, that man's personality is '' grounded in
the Logos,'' he comes near to the Scotist view that the Incarnation
would have taken place even apart from human sin. The Incarnation '' had a relation to the whole plan of the world and not
simply to sin'': it is the pivot on which Creation, with sin foreseen, was built. But he is not a Scotist *simpliciter*; rather does
he link the Scotist position with that which is essentially Thomist,
when he says that in God's one plan for the world, from creation
onwards, the Incarnation has '' immediate reference to Redemption, but it has at the same time a wider scope.'' Orr's emphasis
upon the significance of the Incarnation in itself is seen in his
statement that the Incarnation took place for '' the perfecting
of humanity,'' as also in his sympathetic attitude towards the
belief in the redemptive character of the Incarnation, which is
to be found in Irenæus and Athanasius. This, however, involved
no subordination of the importance of our Lord's death. He is
typical of Scottish theologians in his unwillingness to posit the
fact of the Atonement while adopting an agnostic attitude in
respect of theory. The fact, he holds, must be capable of
assimilation by our thought. The Christian doctrine of redemption has as its starting-point, on the human side, the reality of
the sin and guilt of the world, '' which would remain facts,
though the third chapter of Genesis never had been written.''
In the development of his argument, he makes his belief in the
truth of the chapter in question depend upon his belief in sin
and redemption.

At the same time, his aversion from the evolutionary theory
in its bearing on human origins, so noticeable in the much later
work, *Side-Lights on Christian Doctrine* (1909), is already apparent;

9

if its idea of man's beginnings were proved, then, he continues,
" I admit that it would profoundly modify our whole conception
of the Christian system." What he tried to show was that the
findings of scientists, in so far as they were securely based, came
far short of the point where such a modification would be
necessary. His prolonged discussion of the whole subject appears
in *God's Image in Man and its Defacement in the Light of Modern
Denials* (1905), where he concludes that antagonism between
evolution, "when . . . restricted within the limits which the
best-established results of science at the present hour seem to
impose upon it," and the Biblical view of man's origin largely
vanishes. It is, of course, open to question whether what may
be a strong apologetic position at one time will always remain so.
It is certain that many Protestant theologians, who would not,
any more than Orr, rank as "liberals," do not bind up their
doctrine of man, sin, and redemption with a rejection of the
view that man is to be included within the evolutionary process.
Reinhold Niebuhr's recent Gifford Lectures on *The Nature and
Destiny of Man* (1945) do not directly discuss the question, but
there can, I think, be no doubt as to where he stands.

Orr's doctrine of the Atonement centred in the conception of
Christ's death as a sacrifice, of which " the nerve and core "
was the holy will of the offerer. His interpretation of the
resurrection of man's body is that " the organic, constructive
principle " endures after death. As to final consequences he was
no universalist, but those who would differ from him here could
hardly fail to recognize the judicious and well-balanced manner
in which he discusses the problem. Characteristic of his outlook
are the words which are to be found in one of his last and most
conservative works, *Side-lights on Christian Doctrine*: " We
may be absolutely certain that the mercy of God will reach
as far as ever it is possible for it to reach." It is a certainty
in which the minds and hearts of many Christians, be they
" theologians " or not, will be content to rest.

Orr was not a Protestant scholastic divine after the manner
of Turretin in the seventeenth century and his own American
contemporary B. B. Warfield. Yet he is reminiscent of the
tradition which they represented. That was not the case with
his eminent colleague James Denney, in mind and character
one of the most gifted and influential Scotsmen of his day. As a

New Testament scholar and commentator he was in the first rank; as an expounder of the doctrine of the Atonement he was Dale's superior in exact understanding of the text of the Gospels and Epistles; and if he lacked Forsyth's distinctive vision of the *theologia crucis*, as that in which the revelation of God in Christ was summed up and its moral meaning secured, he possessed a clarity both of thought and style which made his writings far easier to understand. He was an able and caustic, sometimes too caustic, critic. He had a particular dislike of theories and speculations in which, as he judged, the New Testament was wrested to say and mean what it neither meant nor said. Doubtless he was unduly unsympathetic towards points of view not naturally his own; but the astringent quality of his comments was not the sign of a narrow-minded conservative who did his work in blinkers.

Denney was one of those teachers and leaders whom no label fits. He was a Church leader in a way that Bruce never was, but it is, I think, impossible to conceive of him as handling any case after the manner of Rainy, who unquestionably was a great Church leader, and that whether one does or does not approve of Rainy's action in the Robertson Smith case. Anyone who wishes for an inside view, so far as that is possible, of this remarkable man should read the volume which contains letters of his written over many years to William Robertson Nicoll, and the companion volume of letters edited by Professor Moffatt. He will realize that Denney's interests were far from being confined to theological and ecclesiastical matters. His humanism was, perhaps, not as definitely integrated with his Christianity as was Forsyth's. Yet few indeed have been the theologians of the Reformed, or of any, tradition who could say that if the historical plays of Shakespeare were to be lost, their memories could restore them: doubtless an exaggeration, but a revealing one.

Denney's most important books are three in number: *The Death of Christ* (1902), with which now is bound up what may be called an explanatory sequel, *The Atonement and the Modern Mind* (1903); *Jesus and the Gospel* (1908); and *The Christian Doctrine of Reconciliation*, Cunningham Lectures of 1917, published after Denney's death. In the first and the last books he put his full powers as an interpreter of the New Testament and as a theologian

to the task of showing what the atoning work of Christ meant
for the New Testament writers, how it has been construed by
great Christian thinkers, and what are the fundamental truths
concerning it which the Church can never abandon. Even more
than to Orr the distinction between the fact of the Atonement and
a theory thereof was a thoroughly unsatisfactory one to Denney.
Of course neither of them implied that the saving power of the
Cross of Christ was dependent upon a right conception of the
nature of the Atonement. But a fact to which no definite meaning
was attached seemed to them to lack all significance. One may
say that the question to which Denney thought it most necessary
to try to give an answer was the question, What did Christ do,
both for His Father and for men, when He died on the Cross ?

The answer that Denney gave was that Christ stood in our
place and bore the just condemnation of our sins. In doing so
He fulfilled the will of God, who revealed His love for sinful men
by sending His Son to die for them, and thereby to do for them
what they could never do for themselves. This is, in substance,
the doctrine of penal substitution, as it was taught by Lutheran
and Reformed theologians in the sixteenth and seventeenth
centuries and by most of their successors. Denney strongly
defended the word " substitute " as applied to Christ; it seemed
to him to safeguard, as the word " representative " did not, the
truth that Christ was not put forward by man, but was given
by God to and for man. Nor could Denney have repudiated the
adjective " penal." He could not have done so while he held that
sin deserved to be punished, that death had a spiritual significance
and was not a natural event so far as man was concerned, and that
Christ bore for sinners what they deserved to bear.

Dr. G. B. Stevens in *The Christian Doctrine of Salvation* (1905)
argues that Denney's Lectures reprinted in *The Atonement and
the Modern Mind* showed important changes in his doctrine, and,
indeed, that they represented an essentially different point of
view. I cannot think that he makes out his case. What Denney
wished to make plain was that he did not view the Atonement as
a kind of legal transaction involving notions of quantitative
comparison—so much sin, so much punishment, and of retribu-
tive justice as possessing the primacy among the divine attributes.
Some theologians have come very near to such positions, but
such categories of thought were alien to Denney.

It would, however, be true to say that in *The Christian Doctrine of Reconciliation* there is a change of atmosphere. That is due mainly to the stress that falls upon love. Denney had not then learnt for the first time the truth of Hugo of St Victor's *non quia reconciliavit amavit, sed quia amavit reconciliavit*. Yet in the earlier books there is no such manifest insight into the wonder and power of love, into God's saving grace as the fruit of His love, as is here revealed. The old Denney had not passed away: no one who values theological work free from all amateurishness and airy fancies could wish that he had; but something, some liberation of feeling, had made it possible for him to make the love of God the principal theme, to proclaim its omnipotence, as he had never done before.

" It is not sin which is the last reality in the world. . . . The last reality is beyond sin. It is a love which submits to all that sin can do, yet does not deny itself, but loves the sinful through it all. . . . We do not preach that Jesus died, but that He died for us, and in particular that He died for our sins. . . . There is no simpler way of describing the effect of His death than to say that it dispels the despairing conviction that for us sin is the last of all things, in which we must hopelessly acquiesce, and evokes the inspiring conviction that the last of all things is sin-bearing love, through which the sinner may be reconciled to God."

Denney, like Orr, was very critical of the Ritschlian theology, a subject which brought him into controversy with Dr. Garvie, whose attitude was one of judicious sympathy, though by no means of whole-hearted agreement. To Denney, not less than to Orr, Ritschl's rejection of natural theology and aversion from metaphysics in relation to religious truth was uncongenial. In one of his earlier writings, *Studies in Theology* (1894), he makes his position plain. " Is it," he asks, " a wise or right thing . . . to discredit the arguments by which the human mind has sought to explain its belief in God on other grounds, and to deny them either place or consideration in theology ?" He has in mind other grounds besides the knowledge of God as the God and Father of our Lord Jesus Christ. Religious certainty cannot, he protests, be built on " indifference to reason or scepticism of it."

This book of Denney's contains also a clear and valuable exposition of the Incarnation and of the relation of the divine and human in the Person of Christ. Denney was as little likely as a theologian can be to ignore the distinction between God and man. But he would not have been prepared to accept as adequate the acknowledgment by Barth, quoted by Dr. Niebuhr from Barth's reply to Brunner in *Nein*, that man is not a cat. Again, in agreement with Orr, Denney looks to the Logos doctrine for the explanation of human personality, with consequences that follow in respect of the personality of Christ. "All human personality," he says, "we are led to think, is rooted in the Logos, and the Logos made flesh could be the personal centre not of a life alien to man, but of a life truly and purely human." This conviction he expresses still more definitely in the words: "There is no *mere* man in the world, in the sense of a man whose nature is entirely alien to God, out of relation to the Divine; but the completeness with which God is present in Christ depends upon a unique incarnation." This belief that the Divine incarnate in Christ is "at least essentially akin to man" confirms his denial of inconsistency between personality in the Logos and in a truly human life: "In whatever sense personality is to be ascribed to the Word, that same personality is the centre of the life which began at Bethlehem." It is in no pantheistic sense, and not quite after the manner of the patristic doctrine of the *communicatio idiomatum*, that he affirms that in Christ the divine is human, the human is divine. But, in general, his Christology is that of the Council of Chalcedon, and he defends the definition.

This close adherence to the form of the orthodox doctrine does not continue in the later book *Jesus and the Gospel* (1908). Of it one may say that it is hard not to feel a real lack of harmony between the last chapter and all that goes before. The main substance of the volume is a highly impressive exposition of and argument for the thesis contained in the sub-title, "Christianity Justified in the Mind of Christ." The appeal is to our Lord's words in the synoptic Gospels, as words of One whom they reveal as knowing Himself to be Messiah and Son of God, and as asking for a trust and obedience, for a following of Himself, otherwise unaccountable and unjustifiable. This was, of course, not a new appeal or argument, but Denney was able to present it in a way that brought out its great strength. Everything pointed to a reaffirmation of the historic Christianity with which, and not with any other doctrinal form, the result of Denney's study of the Gospels was unquestionably consonant. But for some reason, not clearly manifest, Denney had, apparently, reacted against any Christological form. He had not become " unorthodox," but he seems to have reached the conclusion that no doctrinal statement was adequate to express the truth involved in the Gospel picture of Christ. He will have nothing good to say of the Arian position, but of the Athanasian he remarks, almost complainingly, that it explains nothing. That Denney had come to hold any kind of " reduced Christology " would be a conclusion quite incompatible with the book as a whole and with all other evidence. The chapter presents a problem more puzzling than Bruce's *Encyclopædia Biblica* article; for there was an aspect of Bruce's earlier work that looks in that direction.

Studies in Theology (1894) consists of a course of lectures on Christian doctrine given in America, and is the one book that shows Denney's powers as a systematic theologian. In one chapter he speaks of the new life that came into being through the Gospel, and gives expression to his sense of one splendid vacancy in it in words that deserve quotation. " There is not," he says, " in the New Testament from beginning to end, in the record of the original and genuine Christian life, a single word of despondency or gloom," a note that he strikes again in *Gospel Questions and Answers* (1896), when he writes of the New Testament's characteristic note being " joy in a life which leaves nothing to be desired." At the same time, Denney was unable to construe the Gospel as one of universal optimism concerning man's destiny. It is characteristic of him that he brings to the consideration of final issues the test of his own responsibility and possible failure: " I dare not say to myself that if I forfeit the opportunity this life offers I will ever have another; and therefore I dare not say so to another man." It is the same possibility of his own personal loss which, in the last sentence of the chapter entitled " The Destiny of the Individual " in the first volume of his Gifford Lectures, Professor A. E. Taylor affirms that he has no right to ignore.

Denney's competence was manifold, but it is in the field of the New Testament, as exegete, commentator, and theologian, that his great powers were most fruitfully employed. Severely critical of theorizings that seemed to him to rest upon no secure foundations, his attitude was less conservative than Orr's. A comment of his in connexion with the Robertson Smith case shows a definite rejection of any doctrine of verbal inerrancy, and he makes that clear in *Studies*. With Genesis i-iii. in mind he affirms that myth, as belonging to a pre-scientific, prehistorical age, " may be made the medium of revelation." But, apart from what he wrote in this comparatively early work, he never gave considered attention to the doctrine of Holy Scripture, to what is meant when the Bible is declared to be the Word of God. One cannot but regret, especially in view of modern discussions on this very point, that Denney never made the contribution to this subject which he was so well qualified to give.

With Principal George Galloway of St. Andrews we return to that sphere of the philosophy of religion which Dr. Flint so greatly adorned. Dr. Galloway's work shows considerable difference from that of the Edinburgh professor. It is in less close touch with the theology of the Church, less concerned with the consolidation of positions from which that theology can move forward. His philosophical interests did not lead him to favour what he regarded as the intrusion of metaphysics into religion, an event to which the formulated doctrines of the Church seemed to him to bear witness. In contrast with this, his emphasis falls not upon the Bible but upon the religious consciousness and religious experience. In Flint the Biblical theologian *latet*, if not *patet*, beneath the philosopher: one could not say that of Galloway. This should not, however, be taken to mean that Christianity was for him no more than one form of the expression of the general religious consciousness. The development of the argument in *Faith and Reason in Religion* (1927) shows that that was by no means the case. There he does indeed claim an authority for religious experience, which dogmas that have developed out of it cannot share. " It is only within the life of religion itself that its ground in Reality is felt and experienced. Therefore to establish vital contact with religion on its inner side is the condition of its right appreciation." He asks whether there is anything absolute and ultimate in the Christian experience, and derives his reply from the fact of Jesus Christ as a supreme and creative personality, " whose Spirit has decisively influenced human history as no other has done." So " in Christ God turns directly to man," and Christianity regarded as the supreme expression of the Divine Spirit entering into human history is

absolute and final.   The theological interpretation of this fact
may change, but the reality abides. To this fact of the revelation
of God in Jesus Christ, Christian experience is vitally related.

A similar emphasis upon religious experience, with a critical
attitude to dogmatic theology, appears in *Religion and Modern
Thought* (1922).   He writes with approval of the Ritschlian
effort " to liberate theology from a dead weight of dogma and
to bring it into a living relation with religious experience."
Yet his attitude to dogma is not marked by the pessimism
characteristic of Hatch and Harnack.   He does not regard the
ancient creeds as evidence of a Christianity that had lost its
true and original religious spirit; his dissatisfaction with them
is based upon his belief that they are no longer adequate expressions of the " growing spiritual consciousness."   Of what he
regards as the metaphysical propositions concerning the Trinity
and the Person of Christ he says that they cannot be shown to
be " vitally related to our spiritual faith."   In *The Philosophy
of Religion* (1914) the same aversion from metaphysics in theology
as the Ritschlians displayed is visible: theology should not
develop metaphysical theories, " for they stand in no direct
and vital relation to the religious experience and the spiritual
values of the religious life."   The speculative problems of
religion should be reviewed in connexion with the philosophy
of religion.

It is obvious that these judgments open out a wide field of
controversy.   The accrediting of religious experience as the
substance of religion and as the sufficient test of religious truth;
the sharp distinction urged as existing between such experience
and metaphysical theories; the criticism of dogma as involving
the importation of those theories into religion—need strict
examination before their stability can be admitted. Dogmatic
theology, in anything like the historic sense of the words, seems
entirely to disappear between religious experience and the
philosophy of religion, whereas it is at least conceivable that
some of those speculative problems which Galloway would
hand over to the philosophy of religion may be, if not solved,
yet illuminated by contributions that only dogmatic theology
can make. And when in *Religion and Modern Thought* he is thinking of the eternal life of God before creation, or, more precisely,
of God as " the eternally creative ground of the world and

finite spirits,'' it is to the Logos-doctrine and to the scriptural
revelation of God as Love that he turns. But this, hardly less
than the doctrine of the Trinity, to which Flint refers in a similar
context, takes Galloway on to ground which the dogmatic
theologian, who starts from a definite creed, can much more
reasonably claim as his own than could any philosopher of religion.

As a religious philosopher, Galloway has the idealistic tradition
as the background of his work, but he is independent of any
particular master; he is perhaps nearer to the English personal
idealists than to any other group. He denies that God should
be identified with the philosophic Absolute. God, he affirms
in *The Philosophy of Religion*, is the Absolute, as the sole and
sufficient reason for the world's existence, and His consciousness
is of the whole universe, but He is not the Absolute as though
He were identical with the universe: '' the universe as a system
is the Absolute, and God is not identical with the universe.''
God is personal, creative, Spirit; on Him, as the one supreme
teleological will, finite centres depend for their existence and
order, but that does not involve for Galloway a belief that in
God no change of any sort may be predicated. On the contrary,
'' no mind is conceivable, whether human or divine, which
does not imply states of consciousness that change. A God
absolutely removed from change might be an impersonal
substance: he could not be a living and spiritual God.'' This
same notion of change in relation to the Divine mind appears
in *The Idea of Immortality* (1919). Here the argument develops
along philosophical lines, with the conservation of values seen
in close relation to personal life. '' Persons,'' he writes, '' are
the creators and sustainers of the world of values, and the realms
of ethics and spiritual religion are the outcome of personal
life.'' He builds confidently upon what he finds given through
the moral sense: '' To distrust the working of my moral consciousness is as subversive as to distrust the working of my
intellect: in the end it leads to sheer scepticism.'' His confidence
in the truth of universal salvation springs from the philosopher's
conviction that in the end there must be a manifested unity,
though one should add that the conviction is of an ethical rather
than of a purely speculative character. His denial that there can
be '' an abiding dualism at the heart of things,'' which would
involve two kingdoms of light and darkness in eternal contrast

and antagonism, leads on to the positive assertion that "the divine redeeming purpose must be achieved, and evil cannot finally resist the transforming power of divine goodness."

With his belief in immortality coheres his conception of the transcendent world in *Religion and the Transcendent* (1930). It is a "realm which transcends the mundane form of experience and is therefore not reducible to it." Spatial and temporal representations do not apply to that order. Space and time have no relevance to the transcendent ground of the universe, a view, it may be remarked, which does not seem to go quite easily with the doctrine of changing states of consciousness in the divine mind, particularly as for Galloway the causal order is one in space and time, which a higher order qualitatively transcends. Where New Testament scholars, and theologians who depend on the New Testament far more directly than is the case with Galloway, would agree with him is in his description of the Christian idea of eternal life as one in which "quantitative extension in time no longer counts." Whether this life means for its possessors an absorption into God or eternal individual existence he regards as possibly beyond our power to say, "unless we are prepared to invoke authority and tradition."

Here Galloway does much less than justice to his own emphasis upon religious experience in its Christian form. In that experience the reality of communion with God is a primary affirmation. It has an immediate relation to belief in the value of the human soul, and in man as child or son, not merely creature. Of all that is given in this experience absorption means the end, while the tendency of the notion that the soul is merged in God is towards a pantheistic rather than a theistic doctrine, a tendency which in *Religion and Modern Thought* he thinks of Christian experience as checking. On which side of the alternatives which Galloway presents the New Testament stands, there can be no doubt at all. The whole picture of God's dealings with man to be found therein is quite incompatible with a doctrine that rules out personal immortality. To lay stress on that is not to appeal in a rigid or mechanical way to authority or tradition, but to recognize that the form of the Christian hope is in line with all that is characteristic of Christian religion as we find it from the first. Had Galloway paid more attention to this, he might have been less critical of doctrines and been less inclined to regard

them as a heritage of very doubtful value, representing the dead
hand of a bygone age.

The gap between philosophy of religion and theology, so
obvious in the work of Galloway, is quite absent from the writings
of his Edinburgh contemporary, Hugh Ross Mackintosh. This
was neither because of a lack of interest in the metaphysical
side and problems of religion, nor because, so far as his books
bear witness, he had arrived at an exact discrimination between
the scope and subject-matter of the two studies. But Mackintosh
would have found it unnatural to approach any religious questions,
however speculative, except by attention to the guidance given
in Scripture. His orthodoxy was rooted in Scripture; to pass
outside of the control of the Word of God in the Bible, and to
treat as outside the range of Scripture problems to which,
whether definitely or by implication, it claimed to possess the
solution, would have seemed to him an essentially unreasonable
course. But with his scriptural orthodoxy Mackintosh combined
the generous interests of a receptive and sensitive mind. He was
well qualified to appraise the value of modern theological movements, and to discriminate between the truth that was being
affirmed or reaffirmed and the form in which expression was
given to it. He was not an original thinker; he was not forceful
in the way that both Bruce and Denney were. But he knew
very thoroughly what any preacher or teacher must be specially
concerned to maintain in respect of the Christian Gospel, and
what he knew, that he was able very clearly to expound.

We have seen that the Scottish theologians have devoted
much thought to the subject of revelation and to man's capacity
for the knowledge of God. Mackintosh made his position, and
his attitude to the views of others, clear in two of his latest
books, *The Christian Apprehension of God* (1929) and *Types of
Modern Theology* (1937). In the former he claims St. Paul in
support of the belief that non-Christians enjoy divine revelation;
men "recognize God's invisible being through His visible
works; they recognize His voice in conscience." He is also
insistent on the objective character of the knowledge of God
possessed by faith; because that is so, the cottager at prayer is as
sure of God as the most learned theologian. In the latter book
he examines the teachings of notable thinkers, beginning with
Schleiermacher. Towards him he is decidedly more sympathetic,

though far from uncritically so, than is Brunner in *Die Mystik und das Wort* (1928). He argues that by his famous " feeling of dependence " Schleiermacher probably meant a mode of objective apprehension, not a merely subjective state; yet he realizes the presence of an ambiguity, and notes how the modern use of the term " experience " has " the air of setting the religious experient free from all dependence on Divine revelation." Mackintosh makes an illuminating comment upon the difficulty of a positive verdict upon Schleiermacher, when he compares him with F. D. Maurice as one who might be said to have a bias against " all existing forms of opinion."

He has much to commend and to criticize in Kierkegaard. With the stress that the latter laid on " existential " thinking Mackintosh had no quarrel: his interpretation of it is that " to think existentially . . . is to think not as a spectator of the ultimate issues of life and death, but as one who is committed to a decision upon them." On the other hand he cannot accept Kierkegaard's statement that God is the " absolutely unknown." Holding, as *The Christian Apprehension of God* makes plain, to the belief that human personality affords the one possible mirror of God, he will not allow that that mirror has been shattered; the Bible suggests that the image of God in man has been " broken yet not utterly destroyed." With Denney, to whom in this connexion he refers, he refuses to " define human and Divine by contrast with each other," and to affirm the truth of the idea of " an absolute, intrinsic and impenetrable dualism as between God and man." Nor was Mackintosh favourably disposed to what he regarded as a " crucifixion of intelligence " asserted by Kierkegaard as the condition for entrance into the Kingdom of God. His attitude to Karl Barth proceeds along the same lines: very appreciative of the positive gains involved in Barth's teaching concerning the particularity of the divine self-revelation in Christ and the doctrines of grace, he could not accept the account of the " one-way relation " between God and the world, with the world regarded as always " over against God." Nor does he find Barth self-consistent in his early theology of the Church. Yet it is worth noting that he remarks of Barth that for him, " as for the greatest minds in the evangelical tradition, it holds true that outside the Church there is no salvation."

To three other works of Dr. Mackintosh I would make brief

reference. The first is *The Doctrine of the Person of Jesus Christ*
(1912) in the International Theological Library. As a comprehensive survey of the history of Christological doctrine,
which is followed by an attempt to keep the full substance of
the Catholic doctrine without the whole terminology in which
it was expressed, it is of great ability and importance. I do not
believe that Dr. Mackintosh made out his case against the Two
Natures' formula as expressed in the Definition of Chalcedon.
That Council does not appear to me to commit the Church to
anything that can properly be called either a metaphysic or a
psychology. But there are those who think it did. They will
realize from Dr. Mackintosh's pages that no Christological re-
statement can rightly represent the Christian Gospel, unless it
fully affirms what, without question, Chalcedon did in its
terminology affirm, that Jesus Christ was truly and completely
both God and Man.

A volume of the year 1915 should not go unnoticed. *Immortality and the Future* well represents Mackintosh's theological insight
and his refusal to speculate beyond the limits given in the New
Testament. He looks forward to a climax of history, which will
be the close of history, "mediated through a final revelation
of what Jesus is." With this passage that connects the end, and
therefore the interpretation of history, with the manifestation of
the truth about Jesus, may be compared a much later one in
Types of Modern Theology, which is also concerned, though along
a different route, with the relation between the Person of Jesus
and history. There Mackintosh challenges the view that the
normal assumptions of what history is are adequate to the
interpretation of Christ as He is in the Gospels. "We have,"
he continues, "to think harder about the problem, which has
no parallel because it is the only one in its class—how the eternal
can be present and be recognized in the temporal." The expec-
tation of a not distant coming of the Lord, as held in the primitive
Church, is set in its right context when Mackintosh speaks
of it as conditioned "by the knowledge of the Lord's perpetual
nearness in the sovereign power of His resurrection." Universal
salvation he could not assert, since "the teaching of Jesus,
as we have it, consistently affirms the finality and permanence
of future punishment."

Mackintosh, like Denney, had a deep sense of the Christian

Gospel's character of joy. There is a remarkable passage in his *Sermons*, published posthumously in 1938, with a memoir of his life prefixed, with which we may take leave of one who was described at Oxford, when he received the degree of D.D. in 1929, as " *inter Scoticos theologos, qui nunc exsistunt, primus, pæne dixerim, inter pares.*" The title of the Sermon is " Wonder and Religion." " Have you ever asked yourself what effect it would have on your outlook upon life, if to-morrow morning you were somehow to make the discovery that the Gospel had nothing in it ? Do we realize that everything would be altered, and that we never could recover the old joy or serenity or power to help others ?" Contrariwise, if in Jesus God has shouldered our burden of sin, weakness, and sorrow, " then there is more in Christ to make us glad than there can be anywhere else to make us sorry."

W. P. Paterson, Professor of Divinity in the University of Edinburgh, delivered in 1924 and 1925 Gifford Lectures which were published under the title of *The Nature of Religion*. In the opening pages he shows himself representative of the tradition we have constantly met with in Scottish theologians, which refuses to regard man, even though fallen, as wholly debarred from all knowledge of God. He calls attention to the fact that the Reformed Church, unlike the Lutheran, " has held that the light of nature guarantees a knowledge of the fundamental truths of religion and morality." He himself argues against the view that no evidence in support of the existence of God the Creator can be derived from nature, man, and history. To the Reformed tradition, with its stress alike upon the sovereignty of God, manifested in the laws and decrees which are the expression of His righteous though inscrutable will, and upon the graciousness of His saving purposes sealed in the promises of the Gospel, is due also the absence in representative Scottish theologians of any sense of strain between the operation in general, without discrimination of individuals, of the laws whereby earthly life is governed and the particularity of God's blessings in individual cases.

Paterson gives admirable expression to the implications of this tradition in the first part of the Gifford Lectures. " There is," he writes, " a widespread, deep-seated conviction—which is supported by much evidence—to the effect that notwithstanding the reign of law, there is still a God of Providence, who is able to act in and through natural causes as the controller and disposer of all events, and whose guiding purpose is the highest good of the soul that puts its trust in Him.'' This conviction as to the care that God has for the individual life must lead on to a conception of such a relation between the will and providence of God and human life as a whole as makes it impossible to describe the course of history truly, if it is completely secularized and regarded as expressive, wholly and solely, of human and sub-human forces. Paterson may go too far in saying that a Philosophy of History is not possible, '' unless account is taken of divine purpose and of a divine will,'' which works towards an end and overrules human design. A Philosophy of History in terms of pure immanentism is not only conceivable: it has been brought into existence. But that such a system of thought is in any real sense rational, that it explains intelligibly what it describes, is at least open to grave doubt. In so far as Paterson meant that human history, shut up into itself and lacking all higher direction, was a futility to which no meaning could, in the end, be ascribed, he was on strong ground.

Paterson, as we have seen, held to the capacity of man for knowledge of God. Neither he nor other Scottish theologians were generally inclined to find that capacity realizing itself exclusively through rational deductions from observed phenomena, nor, on the other hand, exclusively through religious experience. Their sense of the wholeness and fullness of religion kept them from any tendency to narrow the channel of man's advance towards this supreme knowledge. Paterson draws attention to the unwillingness of Scottish thinkers to find in any one element of human nature the special organ for the appreciation of the appeal of religion. '' It was characteristic,'' he writes of Scottish theology from Scougal's *Life of God in the Soul of Man* (1677) to Flint's *Theism*, '' to hold that religion has engaged the personality in the whole range of its powers, and has not been an affair mainly of the intellect, of the heart or of the will.'' He refers in this connexion particularly to Principal Galloway. He rightly observes that '' there are fashions in Apologetics, because of the changing fashions of the age to which it has to address itself,'' and looks forward to the possible rehabilitation of the argument from prophecy. This is in line with his belief, " as is commonly held by the theist," that the future is known to God. Finally, there is a passage in the Gifford Lectures worth quotation if only because of its striking dissimilarity to everything that we should recognize as Barthian. The subject is the world's need and the satisfaction of it. Paterson declares that " at the present stage it is difficult to think of a better gift that could be made to the world than to raise up a great body of men, who, believing in God with all their minds, should make it the governing and passionate purpose of their lives that God's Kingdom may come, and His will be done, in earth as it is in Heaven."

These Gifford Lectures do not point to a mind of great metaphysical power and analytical subtlety. But, as is common with the Scots, Paterson leaves the impression of one whose knowledge and common sense were always adequate to the argument as he developed it. His critical comments are shrewd, but he does not lack the power to appreciate positions with which he is not in agreement. In an earlier volume of Baird Lectures, published under the title of *The Rule of Faith* (1912), he states with admirable clearness the main positions of Christian orthodoxy. Yet, in distinction from what would generally be found in similar books of Anglican writers, it would appear that, in regard both to the substance and to the authority of the Christian creed, a choice must be made between Rome and Geneva. On the whole, the Scottish theologians, to a much greater extent than English ones, recognize two and only two chief dogmatic traditions; neither the conception of a *via media* in dogma, nor an approach to particular dogmas along the lines of an investigation of the nature of dogma and of its relation to the Church, has received much attention in Scottish theology. Galloway might have contributed much at this point, had he not taken too easily and too strongly what seemed to him to be a radical difference between the value of dogma and the value of the experience on which it was based.

The kind of Modernism in relation to dogma which has received not a little support in the Church of England has had very little representation in Scotland. There is a glance that way in Professor W. A. Curtis' Inaugural Lecture at the beginning of the 1903-4 session in the University of Aberdeen. In it he calls attention, first, to " what may be described as unanimous recognition " by the General Assembly of the Church of Scotland that the doctrine, in detail, of the Westminster Confession, " can no longer be claimed to represent the spontaneous beliefs of the great majority of our teachers and preachers," and then to the more rapid change of opinion in the United Free Church as having found " a faltering expression in declaratory resolutions." Like so many others among contemporary Scottish theologians he recognizes the rights and place of reason, which, being " the principle of science and philosophy, has a home in Religion." Reason is " the intelligent principle of human consciousness." It is in his outlook on the future that Curtis takes a line of greater independence. He anticipates a drawing together of men of different religions, Jews, Mohammedans and others, on the basis of admiration for Jesus Christ, when it is clearer that the doctrine of the Trinity is monotheistic, and not " a sort of refined tritheism." And as to the Person of Christ, he holds that men will grow towards an agreement in putting " the same broad construction upon His personality, as related both to God and to man," though that may involve variations from the terms used in the Creeds or even from St. Paul. The nature of the " broad construction " and of the " variations " required more exact description, if a judgment upon the change, as one of substance or only of form, were to be possible. And valuable as Professor Curtis' later large book, *A History of Creeds and Confessions of Faith* (1911), was for the student of formularies, it did not follow further upon the road which the Inaugural Lecture had brought into view.

Of special importance in connexion with Christian apologetics has been the work of another Aberdeen professor, D. S. Cairns. He has not set himself to a comprehensive statement of the case for theistic and Christian belief, with corresponding criticism of the other side, after the manner of A. B. Bruce. But with the interest in the world and life that proclaims the humanist he combines a singular power of showing how the world gains in intelligibility and value when seen in the light of Christian faith. The persuasive note is as noteworthy in his writing as the wooing note was said to be in Dr. J. H. Jowett's preaching. This persuasiveness of his was naturally adapted to the religious and theological climate of the age to which he appealed, and the changes which have affected that climate since his first considerable work, *Christianity in the Modern World*, appeared in 1906 would, to some extent, be unfavourable to the effectiveness of his arguments. The manner of his insistence upon the fact of the historical Jesus and of His teaching, though with an appreciation of the vital and deep distinction between " Christ as simply Interpreter and Christ as Interpreter and Mediator; between Christ as simply Revealer of new Truth and Christ as ' God manifest in the flesh,' " has affinities with Dr. Glover and even with Harnack, hardly anticipates Dr. C. H. Dodd, and has nothing in common with Barth.

The sharpness of Barth's antitheses is alien to Cairns' mind. In a late book, *The Riddle of the World* (1937), he has an appendix critical of Barth, in which he opposes Barth's denial of general revelation: this, says Cairns, " comes far short of the fuller knowledge which I believe God has given us of Himself; but the knowledge which it gives is real, and all truth is of Him." Nor can he accept the expression " wholly other " of God in relation to man; if He were so, God would be " wholly un-knowable by man." The contrast between this world and the next, between the natural and the supernatural, as something sheerly divisive through the event and force of that supernatural movement from above, on which Barth lays such stress, is, if not abolished, powerfully modified when it is said in the earlier book, " no man who enters truly into the spirit of Jesus can find the world-order alien to his soul." And whereas the preponderating tendency of modern New Testament scholarship has been to emphasize the eschatological nature of the Kingdom of God, Cairns looks to the Sermon on the Mount for the revelation of the real nature of the Kingdom, wherein is contained the revelation of the Father and of the soul and its true life and spiritual blessings.

There is more similarity to Dr. Dodd's present teaching when Cairns in another passage speaks of the Parousia as " at once the Process of the Victory of the Kingdom and its Climax," whereby the transition is made from the earthly to the heavenly world. On the other hand, it is curious to find Cairns saying in 1906 concerning the apocalyptic faith that God in Christ will give to life a new environment nobler than that which exists now, that " if any age should be able to understand that Apocalyptic element it is our own, an age which aspires after a humaner social order and a universal peace." The belief in the permeation of this world with the leaven of a true moral and social order, which was so powerful an influence in the first decade of this century, was something very different from the apocalyptic faith that, past redemption as was the present world-order, God would give to His people a new world in which, but not through any efforts of their own, they would live secure.

Not rarely in the case of the Scottish divines are their theological advances made from a background of strong conviction as to the moral order of the world. This conviction is apparent in Dr. Cairns' book, *The Reasonableness of the Christian Faith* (1918). He affirms his entire agreement with the eminent metaphysician of his own country, A. S. Pringle Pattison, that it is "simply waste of time" to engage in argument about God with a man who rejects the "assumption of the infinite value and significance of human life." He is sure that in facing the moral imperative he is "dealing with a world which is not relative but absolute." This categorical imperative is obviously inexplicable, unless the world itself can be described in moral terms. That is allowed for in Cairns' description of the world as a moral order, its "seeming anarchy" only apparent.

Dr. Cairns' reaction against any idea of the world which would present it as a purposeless mechanism is seen at its strongest in his remarkable discussion of the question of the miraculous in *The Faith that Rebels* (1928). At the centre of his argument concerning the reality and importance of the Gospel miracles is the insistence on the faith that Christ had in the almighty Father, His assurance that in events of the physical order the will of God could be manifested. For Cairns miracle, as it is met with in the Gospels, is not the guarantee of revelation; it is part of revelation; and one may specially note his reference to the problem of evil as illuminated by the testimony that miracle bears to the overruling power of God. A profound sense of latent resources, usable for ethical and spiritual ends, in nature and human nature, is recognizable in Cairns' work, which is the more impressive because of his ability in combining the temper of the apologist who addresses the mind with that of the evangelist who speaks to the soul. And his power of vivid writing is notably revealed in his imaginative but not fanciful delineation of what led up to our Lord's walking on the sea.

The Scottish divines with whose teaching I have been concerned are to be thought of as of the past, not of the present. However much the influence of some of them continues, they speak in their writings to an age that in various ways, in its presuppositions, outlooks, problems, sense of values, differs considerably from our own. Except in the case of the greatest thinkers and writers on religious and theological subjects, we read those of a previous generation rather to learn what they thought than to learn to see with their eyes. Occasionally someone stands out in almost lonely pre-eminence, so that our interest in him is living, not just historic. Not a few have felt that to be true of McLeod Campbell. The tribute paid to *The Nature of the Atonement* by A. B. Macaulay, " a nobler book on the Death of Jesus has in my judgment never been written in any age or language," words that stand in his own soteriological study that bears the title *The Death of Jesus* (1938), find more than a faint echo in the estimates formed by James Denney and by Dr. Carnegie Simpson. But it will not be often that such a verdict comes to be passed on the work of a scholar of former days. The generations as they come and pass have to discover their own particular teachers, and in this partial survey of some of those who have declared and interpreted the Gospel of Christ to Scotland, I come in a few closing pages to men who are of to-day and to-morrow, and take some account of the nature of their doctrine.

Professor Paterson was succeeded in the chair of divinity at the University of Edinburgh by Dr. John Baillie, who was already known beyond academical circles by writings of a fresh and arresting character. Dr. Baillie is, indeed, a singularly independent thinker, and both those who read him now, and those who will be in a position some day to assess the value of his work as a Christian theologian, must not expect to follow his arguments and expositions as though he were taking them along familiar routes. Particularly should those, to whom it is natural to conceive of the substance of orthodoxy as expressed in a form consecrated by tradition and by its history through the centuries, remember that the fact that the form is not used does not mean that the substance is repudiated. The importance of this observation will become clearer in connexion with the doctrine of the Person of Christ.

Dr. Baillie's book, *The Place of Jesus Christ in Modern Christianity*, dates from 1929. In the same year was published his larger work, *The Interpretation of Religion*, of which something must first be said. In it he shows himself far removed from any tendency either to give theology a starting-point in previous philosophical conclusions, or to discriminate sharply between theology and religion. Thus, he insists that the character of philosophies is weightily affected by the presence or absence of religious faith; declares that it is " religion itself " which the modern theologian studies, the one religion which passes from its most primitive expressions to its final expression " in the soul of Jesus Christ "; dissents from the speculative method in theology as having a claim to precedence; and approves what Herrmann said, " in words which might be taken as the first axiom of any true theology," that " the basis of our faith must be grasped in the same independent fashion by learned and unlearned, by each for himself." He will have nothing to do with any writing down of religion as though it were an imperfect and inferior kind of knowledge, and affirms that scientific metaphysics, in the search for a " synoptic view of reality," makes use of religious insight into the nature and meaning of things. His general attitude is not along Barthian lines; his endorsement of Kant's conception of the laws of conduct, as requiring to be given by reason itself as a " pure practical faculty " before they can be regarded as moral, is in harmony neither with Barth nor with Brunner, nor can one imagine either of these theologians speaking of human discovery and divine self-revelation as " complementary sides of the selfsame fact of experience."

At the end of *The Interpretation* Dr. Baillie touches upon the doctrine of the Incarnation, to which he devotes a fuller discussion in the other book to which I have referred. His thought moves along two lines, which for him unquestionably make for an ultimate unity. On the one hand, Christ is the incarnation of divine perfection: in Christ we see " God seeking man "; the Church has always believed that " in the soul of the man of Nazareth, and in His life and death," we have beheld and known " very God of very God." But along with this goes an approval of Frederic Myers' line:

Jesus, divinest when Thou most art man;

while shortly before the words quoted just above he says that to think of God as incarnate in Jesus alone has " never been " the true Christian teaching; but in Jesus God is incarnate supremely. Those who gain the impression of an unresolved dualism from such statements will not find a way out made easier for them by the Christology of *The Place of Jesus Christ in Modern Christianity*. Certain things are quite clear, that Dr. Baillie intends to affirm not an adoptionist doctrine of Christ's Person but an incarnational one; that he cannot accept that way of stating the doctrine which in its exact form goes back to the Council of Chalcedon; that he is not prepared to work out a Christological doctrine from a starting-point in an " ontological " conception of the Trinity. His manner of thought and expression may be better grasped if I quote a somewhat long passage, which is of the nature of a comprehensive statement:

" Jesus Christ is not another name for God, but the name of a Man in whom God was, and through whom God came to meet us. The Presence which indwells in the Christian's soul is always this God whom through Jesus we found. On the other hand, it is not a God whom we can satisfyingly know in any other way than through Jesus; for nowhere else than in Jesus has He been satisfyingly present in our world. Nor, on the other hand, is it Jesus Himself regarded in His separate human selfhood, but only that in Him which was God in Him. This Presence we may variously speak of as God the Father, or as the Holy Spirit, or as the Inward and Living Christ, according as Christian feeling and Christian liturgical use may in different instances dictate."

" That in Him which was God in Him "—the student of the history of doctrine will not be unfamiliar with such language. But it is just at a point like that that the greatest care is needed in any interpretation. We may be quite sure that Dr. Baillie was not intent on reaffirming the doctrine, rightly or wrongly attributed to Nestorius the Patriarch of Constantinople, and to a more eminent theologian Theodore of Mopsuestia, of two persons in Christ, the divine Logos and the human Jesus. What he does say, and very properly, is that in Christ the divine and the human are not identical with one another; and he has the kind of eye that the Antiochene School of scholarship and theology had for the importance of the real humanity of Christ; nor is it wonderful that one who has studied under Herrmann should speak in accents which recall that most impressive of all the Ritschlians. And I can imagine the perplexity that this manner of statement may occasion to some who have looked at the doctrine of the Incarnation in a very different way, taking as their presupposition the life of the Eternal Word " in the bosom of the Father," and following in their thoughts that life come to earth and clothed with a real humanity, which has, however, no independent subsistence apart from the Word. Such as they would not even find it easy to understand William Temple's avowal of his belief that if *per impossibile* the Word were withdrawn from Jesus Christ there would not be nothing left, there would be a man. Dr. Orr was convinced that the Ritschlians were not truly affirming the divinity and incarnation of the Lord Jesus Christ, and certainly they were not affirming either doctrine after the manner of Athanasius, Cyril, or Leo. Nowhere more than in Christology is that problem of form and substance, which Dr. Sanday and N. P. Williams discussed and to which I have referred, more important and more in need of judicious handling. And, to come back to Dr. Baillie, just because one may feel a strangeness about his angle of vision and approach, it is the more necessary not to find in one's own angle the one and only true criterion. On the other hand, it is not true that it all comes to the same thing in the end, and that it does not matter what forms are used, provided that there is the intention of preserving the substance.

Dr. Baillie had previously dealt with the whole subject of religion in his book, *The Roots of Religion in the Human Soul* (1926). In it he discusses theories of religion, and rejects both the exclusively rationalistic and the exclusively romanticist explanations. Of religious experience he remarks that it must already contain some belief as an integral part of its own being, an observation, or warning, that is often much needed. As to the content of religious experience, he says in a single sentence what is equally simple and profound: " I should say myself that the most fundamental and primordial of all religious experiences, and perhaps in a sense the only experience that is, as such, religious, is just the experience of believing, the experience of faith in God, the experience of casting oneself in utter trust upon His love." The same or a similar note occurs in a passage where he shows sympathy with Matthew Arnold's near approach to the identification of religion and morality. Insisting that religion means confidence in the Power behind phenomena he writes: " I take it to be one of the best established facts of universal history that in the hearts of those who seek goodness there grows up a great sense of trust in an Eternal Goodness. That fact, with what follows from it, is all we mean by religion." With Dr. Inge he sees in the Gospel of Christ not *a* religion but religion itself, " in its universal and deepest significance." As in his later work, he points to the consummation of religion " in the soul of Jesus Christ," and to the universal and inclusive character of Christianity he finds witness in the fact that in Christ's teaching concerning life and God there is something which " makes us feel at once that it can be foreign to no human heart."

To the student of different methods, leading to different results, in the sphere of dogmatics, Dr. Baillie must be a figure of more than ordinary interest. He does not link up with some predecessor after the manner of a modern Roman Catholic theologian with St. Thomas Aquinas, of Rashdall with Abelard, and of Karl Barth with Calvin. Too wise to make little of the heritage of past Christian thinking, he has not the almost passionate interest in it which in some thinkers is so unmistakable. He is still more remote in the general cast of his thought from another passion, that for sharp distinctions passing into oppositions, of which one is conscious in Kierkegaard and in Barth. His own passion moves in the direction of the apprehension of real unities: and if Westcott had not written a book with the title *Christus Consummator*, Dr. Baillie might well have chosen it for the expression of his deepest convictions.

An attitude not dissimilar from that of Dr. John Baillie appears in the Kerr Lectures of 1926 of his brother the Rev. D. M. Baillie, which bear the title, *Faith in God and its Christian Consummation* (1927). He also will not allow to " experience " any precedence over faith. He asks how is experience of religion possible except through faith, and the nature of his own answer is contained in the words, " surely all the possible religious experiences which a man may have are in some sense bound up with a believing attitude of his mind," while he appeals to the whole tradition of Christian theology as affirming that " we can never find or touch or experience God except by faith." What amounts to a doctrine of the unity of Christian apperception is involved in his conclusion that " the belief and the experience *are one*." Like his brother he shows in his chapter on the Person of Christ the influence of Ritschl's mode of approach to the doctrine. " It is," he writes, " because men found in Jesus a supreme realization of these " (supreme faith, supreme love, and so on) " that they recognized in Him an Incarnation of the Divine." And while Jesus is not identical with the Father, Christian faith cannot accept any idea of communion with Christ " which was not at the same time a communion with the Father." To deny that would be an equally grave error, " equally alien to the Christian conception of God." His later book, *I believe in God* (1937), strikes a somewhat different note in connexion with man's knowledge of God. Stress falls not on the place of reason nor even simply on faith, but on experience in one particular manner. The true knowledge of God is said to be possible for a soul only in an experience in which the soul is personally challenged. At the same time there are none of the violent contrasts which some modern writers, greatly influenced by the neo-Calvinistic movement, display, and Dr. W. R. Matthews' book, *God in Christian Thought and Experience*, appears in the bibliography without any disparaging comment upon the main lines of the argument there pursued by the Dean of St. Paul's.

So far, in not one of the Scottish theologians with whom we have been concerned has there been any express repudiation of the time-honoured rational arguments, which have aimed at showing that a real, however limited, knowledge of God is open to those who make use of the faculties with which man is endowed. Not one of them would have been willing to stand alongside of Mansel, and condemn man to a dark night of agnosticism concerning God, apart from the light given in revelation. It is, indeed, very remarkable how these inheritors of the tradition that emphasized, to the point, as some would say, of great exaggeration, the corruption of human nature which had resulted from the Fall, divines whose articles of faith were enshrined in the Westminster Confession, a document of living religion in a sense never true of the Thirty-Nine Articles, did not hesitate to claim that, in virtue of his mind and conscience, man could think and speak truly, with whatever ignorances, limitations, and errors, about the existence and nature of God. Not till the year 1937 was this concordant witness definitely and explicitly broken in a work of positive theology: I refer to the Rev. G. S. Hendry's Hastie Lectures then published, with the title *God the Creator*.

It could hardly be regarded as a mature work; if others would add that it was not well-proportioned, it should be remembered, in justice to its author, that what he considered the false proportions of the past were precisely what he desired to challenge and expose. If it was fiercely, it was also bravely controversial; for in his uncompromising attack upon Dr. Matthews, Mr. Hendry ranged himself against a theologian whose reputation, especially in the sphere of the philosophy of religion, was firmly established, the more so because of his singular clarity both of thought and of word, written or spoken. Moreover, profound as had been the interest aroused in the work of Karl Barth, an interest with which there often went a sincere and ready acknowledgment of all that he was doing to bring the theology of the Bible into the centre of attention, and to expound the nature of the Christian Gospel, with consequences of the first importance for teaching as well as for preaching, the sharpness of his antitheses and the impression that he gave of one-sidedness were in themselves sufficient to arouse at the start grave doubts in the minds of men who approached the problems of theology in a very different way. No one who read his book could fail to recognize in Mr. Hendry, if not a Barthian, at least one who conceived of the origin and nature of true religious knowledge in much the same way as the Swiss theologian.

Near the beginning of his Lectures he declares his scepticism as to any "harmonious adjustment" of Hebrew and Greek views in respect of the knowledge of God. He points out that the new movement (that is, the Barthian theological tendency) was convinced that "philosophic thought necessarily leads to a conception of God which is radically incompatible with the knowledge of the God and Father of our Lord Jesus Christ." The knowledge of God resulting from philosophy he describes as "incompetent and futile." It is to revelation alone that we must look, and revelation, as apprehended by Christian faith, does not involve an act of human perception, but is a drawing back of the veil to disclose what otherwise could not be known. God does not present Himself as an object of human thought. Mr. Hendry lays great stress upon the doctrine of grace in its bearing upon the doctrine of God. He affirms its incompatibility

" with any philosophical idea of God," and is nervous in the presence of Augustine's saying that God is the *æterna veritas*, words which seemingly combine religion and philosophy. He is, in fact, as hostile to philosophy as was Luther, and it is Luther's stress upon the approach to God along the road of sin and its forgiveness, and upon the knowledge of God as given in Christ and Christ alone, which he reasserts. And his conclusion is that we are at the end of the period of the acquiescence of theology in its Babylonian captivity to modern thought; that we are once more facing the issues that Luther faced; and that so far as Scottish theology is concerned, its orientation should no longer be towards England but towards the continent and towards that theology of the Reformed Church, with which lies the true spiritual affinity of Scotland.

A much more moderate standpoint is adopted by Dr. E. P. Dickie in his Kerr Lectures for 1937 (*Revelation and Response*, 1938). He does not doubt the value of the neo-Calvinistic movement, but he disapproves its rigour. He will not admit of a sharp dissociation of reason and revelation. " Deny," he says, " the authenticity of reason's judgment, and you make it for ever impossible for man to tell when he has the truth; when God is speaking to him. Irrationalism is in danger of ending in agnosticism." But this does not mean that he has unlimited confidence in the human reason and its powers. Troeltsch he regards as wrong in not recognizing the possibility that in Christianity and the Person of Jesus history " *may* be faced by the inexplicable." One who takes up the attitude of the spectator, in detachment from faith, has not the means adequate to the attainment of truth: and faith he describes as " not perception; it is decision." This account of faith is entirely in line with what Barth has said concerning man's act of self-committal, akin to a leap over a precipice, where nevertheless man is not shattered to pieces, since he is upheld by God.

But Dr. Dickie cannot follow Barth in what he holds to be the exaggeration of " human brokenness." Whereas Barth's doctrine of discontinuity between man and God is as relevant for the denial of a valid approach to God by means of the moral sense as through speculation or mysticism, Dr. Dickie declares that " if there is one certainty in human life it is that God is speaking in conscience." At the same time, he does not disavow Barth's entire doctrine of revelation, but to this extent, apparently, states his agreement with it, that " revelation, if it *is* revelation, is something absolute and ultimate, and therefore not open to testing by anything else whatsoever, except revelation." Whether this is consistent with his earlier strong emphasis upon the " authenticity " of the judgment of reason depends on the exact reference involved in the word " testing." If it were implied that reason could not apply any test to make sure that something which claimed to be of the nature of revelation was such, Dr. Dickie would have come near to a contradiction of his former statement. But if his meaning was that the actual substance of the thing revealed could be tested only by reference to some other admitted point of revelation, no such charge would lie against him. Before I pass from Dr. E. P. Dickie, I would borrow from him a story of point and humour, which the hearers of the Kerr Lectures must have enjoyed, even if any high Calvinists among them may have been shocked. (But as it comes in a note, perhaps it was not adventured in the lecture-room.)

" It is said," he remarks, " that the following answer was once made to the presentation of very strict Calvinist doctrine: ' when the first sin was committed, Adam put the blame on the woman and the woman put the blame on the serpent. The serpent, who was as yet young and dull, made no answer. Now he has become old and confident, and comes to the synod of Dort, and says that God has done it.' "

The liberal orthodoxy characteristic of Dr. Mackintosh's work is the note of Dr. John Dickie's interesting and attractive book, *The Organism of Christian Truth: A Modern Positive Dogmatic* (1931). In his preface he looks back to Dr. Flint in relation to the theory of religious knowledge. After speaking of the Bible as doing its work not as an " indivisible, inerrant whole . . . but through the power of a self-authenticating religious kernel to impress itself on us as divinely authoritative truth," he goes on later to express the opinion that Dr. Flint's " purely intellectualistic view of the nature of religious knowledge and the conditions of theological proof drove many of us—perhaps too far—in other directions " (i.e., as contrasted with a stress upon revelation in the Bible and a response to it). Nevertheless, he continues: " Flint's students must always regard him as in many respects their ideal theologian."

Dr. Dickie's own position becomes clear as he develops his thought as to the Person and work of Christ, and moves forward from the latter to the former doctrine. Like other Scottish divines he shows a profound admiration for McLeod Campbell's book, *The Nature of the Atonement*, which he describes as "epoch-making, as indicating the right spirit and method of approach to the doctrine of our Lord's work," and as showing the close inter-connexion of what Christ is, what He does for us, and what He does in us. He himself offers a very fair criticism of the theory of penal satisfaction. In his discussion of the doctrine of the Incarnation Dr. Dickie finds no difficulty in respect of the limitation of our Lord's knowledge, and sees an over-intellectualistic theory of knowledge in those "who are concerned to maintain our Lord's infallibility with reference to those things which do not affect His true and proper work as our Saviour and Redeemer." The kenotic theology, as expressed in the writings of Dr. Weston of Zanzibar, of Dr. Forsyth and Dr. D. W. Forrest, he much prefers to the older forms of that theory, in affirming "a real self-emptying, but that we are unable to determine its precise limits." On the subject of miracle, Dr. Dickie unhesitatingly believes that the sepulchre was empty on Easter morning, while he does not think that such belief is essential to Christian faith in the Resurrection. As to the Virgin Birth, that also he affirms, but not as the *prius* to belief in Christ, nor as a truth binding upon every Christian. But this is one of the points which show the need for a more considered treatment of the relation of the doctrine of the Church to the faith of the individual Christian.

I have tried to exhibit some of the main features in the teaching of a number of those whose names have their place in the long and distinguished roll of Scottish theologians. Yet in these pages the roll is by no means complete. No mention has been made of Henry Drummond, whose book, *Natural Law in the Spiritual World*, had a great influence in its day, and was of an essentially eirenic character at a time when controversy concerning the bearings of scientific discovery, and, particularly, of the Darwinian theory, upon religion, was marked by a sharpness which did not help towards mutual understanding. In the field of Christology two contributions of note were made by Dr. D. W. Forrest, *The Christ of History and of Experience* (1897) and *The Authority of Christ* (1906). The former is comparable in some respects with Dr. Glover's two volumes, *The Jesus of History* (1917) and *Jesus in the Experience of Men* (1921), but is in much more direct touch with the historic form of Christian orthodoxy. In the latter work Dr. Forrest seeks to show the nature of our Lord's authority, while he does not draw the kind of conclusion which follows when Christ's words are held to be decisive in the spheres of literary and historical criticism. His "kenotic" doctrine is, in relation to the question of Christ's human knowledge, similar to that which Forsyth was afterwards to develop with much more theological subtlety and completeness.

No Scottish divine of recent years has written as much about the Atonement as did Dr. James Denney, but there are others whose work must not be passed over in silence. Dr. A. B. Macaulay has laid stress on the need for a doctrine that shall fit present needs. Even so, he, with Denney, Dr. Carnegie Simpson and others of the Scottish tradition, gives to McCleod Campbell a place of almost solitary eminence. Dr. Macaulay's own conception of Christ's atoning work is, I think it not unfair to remark, more original than convincing. His book, which bears the title of *The Death of Jesus* (1938), hardly conforms to any one type of doctrine. He rejects the theory of penal substitution and finds the "moral-influence" interpretation inadequate. He conceives of "a real encounter of the soul of Jesus with the guilt, malignity and dominion of sin in what McCleod Campbell strikingly describes as ' the perfected personal experience of the enmity of the carnal mind to God '—an encounter conditioned by His perfect sense of the holiness of God, and by His perfect realization of the nature and enormity of sin." And the special trial which Christ faced on the Cross was as to His assurance that His own attitude towards man, His spirit of loving forgiveness, was that of His Father. This, coupled with "a dreadful temptation of His love and faith in man," constituted His ordeal. And what the experience of Christ on the Cross reveals is the divine condemnation of sin and, along with it, the forgiving love of God. Dr. Macaulay's critical attitude to the Apostles' Creed may be noted; he takes exception to certain ambiguities which he finds in it, and concludes that it ought not to continue to be used as a public confession and declaration.

How far the lessened stress upon the rigorous Calvinism of the Westminster Confession will be balanced, among Scottish theologians, by a movement in the direction of the neo-Calvinism of Karl Barth and his associates on the Continent has yet to be seen. One holder of a theological chair, Professor G. T. Thomson, of Edinburgh, is clearly looking in that direction, as his word of introduction to the translation of the first volume of Barth's *Dogmatik* shows. And it is to another Scottish writer, Dr. J. McConnachie, that we owe two books, partly expository and partly defensive, in which Barth's theology is the theme. On the whole, the relations between theology and philosophy have been closer in Scotland than in England, which means a climate of thought unfavourable to any enthusiastic reception of Barth's hostility towards the whole conception of natural theology. On the other hand, Barth's positive interpretation of Christian theology, markedly different from that character-istic either of Catholicism or of liberalism, may make a strong appeal in a country where the roots of the Reformed tradition have gone deep. G. S. Hendry and G. T. Thomson may represent the beginnings of a movement parallel with that which has certainly revivified the Protestant theology of Europe. It might have been expected that the Catholicism of the Scottish Episcopal Church would exercise an influence that would make for a more intimate mutual understanding of the Catholic and the Reformed traditions. So far as I am aware (and I would make all reservations which befit an English writer) that is not, to any considerable extent, the case. There has been a "High Church" tendency in the Church of Scotland in years gone by, with Professor James Cooper as its best-known name, and more attention has been paid in recent years to liturgical worship, but it would be a mistake to lay any great emphasis upon theological implications or results.

The men whose work we have been considering have been professors in the universities or colleges of Scotland. A college not in Scotland, but surely of Scotland, must not be overlooked, Westminster College, Cambridge. Existing for the training of candidates for the Presbyterian ministry, it has been fortunate in the possession of teachers whose worth has not been less than that of their brethren and colleagues in the north. In particular I would refer to that quattuorvirate which for many years adorned its lecture-rooms. Dr. Skinner in Old Testament, Dr. Anderson Scott in New Testament, Dr. Carnegie Simpson in Church History, and Dr. Oman in Dogmatics and the Philosophy of Religion formed a teaching staff such as is very rarely met. Each of them made, and mainly while at Westminster, remarkable contributions to learning and theology. Dr. Skinner applied his Hebrew and Old Testament scholarship to Genesis and Isaiah, Dr. Anderson Scott devoted himself chiefly to St. Paul; Dr. Carnegie Simpson, the biographer of Principal Rainy, became well known in many countries as the author of *The Fact of Christ* (1900), a book most admirably fitted in substance and style to help the reader to feel the wonder of Christ's Person, and so to lead him on to face the great questions involved in Christian doctrine: " Who was Jesus Christ ?", " What did He do ?"

Of Dr. Oman one may say that he became one of the most impressive writers of his day in connexion with the philosophy of religion, and, in particular, the study of man on the religious side. Easy he is not; nor is he always lucid; but he is always going down to the roots of the matter, and he is the enemy *à outrance* of anything that seems to him unreal. His last book, *Honest Religion* (1941), makes it clear what kind of a man he was in his outlook and his teaching. And last though it is, it might form a good introduction to those remarkable works of his maturity, *Grace and Personality* (1917) and *The Natural and the Supernatural* (1931). The former, in particular, is sufficient to place its writer among the most penetrating religious thinkers of his generation. Dr. Oman was greatly concerned to repudiate all notions of an impersonal order, where the relations of God with man were being considered, and the object of his treatment of the controversial questions, that arose in connexion with the Pelagian controversy, was to show how impossible it was to arrive at any true understanding of grace and freedom, so long as conceptions which implied operations on the part of God, in which He viewed men as less than personal, were dominant. The way in which, for Augustine as well as Pelagius, God stood over against man, and the divine action excluded the human and the human action the divine, was for Oman fundamentally wrong. Of course he has not said the last word on this, which is one of the great themes in Christian theology; but he has said a word of such importance that no student of theology ought to be content to leave *Grace and Personality* unread. It belongs to that small class of books, of which Hort's Hulsean Lectures, *The Way, The Truth, The Life*, is an outstanding example, which reveal, as it were, the inner side of religious truth. The following passage, taken from the chapter in *Grace and Personality* entitled " Mechanical Opposites," puts with a clearness to which Oman did not always attain the pith of what he wished to express and contend for, as alone doing justice to God's grace and man's will.

" Religious and moral positions," he writes, " being opposed mechanically, admit of no solution, but, being combined personally, they admit of no conflict. The way of the working of God's gracious personal relation to His children is shown precisely in that reconciliation, which, being on His side the succour of our freedom, and, on ours, the liberty of His children, is not religious in one aspect and moral in another, but is moral because it is religious and religious because it is moral. . . . A right relation to God is at once moral and religious—inseparably one, yet our dependence and our independence cannot be brought into unity by any process of resolving the moral into the religious or the religious into the moral."

Dr. Oman's successor at Westminster College in the sphere of dogmatics and of the philosophy of religion is Dr. H. H. Farmer, whose writings have already attracted considerable attention. He, with Dr. Elmslie, the Principal, and his other colleagues, will aim at maintaining the high standards of scholarship and theology bequeathed to them by their predecessors. Of the Scottish tradition, as a whole, in so far as I have been able to give any adequate account of it, I cannot take leave without expressing my sense of the debt that Christians of other communions owe to its representatives, for all that they have done to uphold and illuminate the truth of the Gospel.

INDEX